RIVER F

DR
P9-DNL-872

31865002319191

WITHDRAWN

TOP 10
MALLORCA

River Forest Public Library
735 Lathrop Avenue
River Forest, IL 60305
708-366-5205
May 2020

Top 10 Mallorca Highlights

The Top 10 of Everything

CONTENTS

Mallorca Area by Area

Streetsmart

Within each Top 10 list in this book, no hierarchy of quality or popularity is implied. All 10 are, in the editor's opinion, of roughly equal merit.

Title page, front cover and spine *The beautiful Camp de Mar coastline*
Back cover, clockwise from top left *Tram at sunset in Sóller; sunset over Port de Sóller; boats in the blue Mallorcan sea; Església de Nostra Senyora dels Dolors, Manacor*

The information in this DK Eyewitness Top 10 Travel Guide is checked regularly. Every effort has been made to ensure that this book is as up-to-date as possible at the time of going to press. Some details, however, such as telephone numbers, opening hours, prices, gallery hanging arrangements and travel information, are liable to change. The publishers cannot accept responsibility for any consequences arising from the use of this book, nor for any material on third-party websites, and cannot guarantee that any website address in this book will be a suitable source of travel information. We value the views and suggestions of our readers very highly. Please write to: DK Eyewitness Travel Guides, Dorling Kindersley, 80 Strand, London WC2R 0RL, Great Britain, or email travelguides@dk.com

Welcome to
Mallorca

Mallorca's breathtaking coastline, with its cobalt coves and glorious beaches, has long been the island's main attraction, enhanced by year-round sunshine. But there is more to Mallorca than its coast: it also boasts the spectacular Serra de Tramuntana mountains, the charming and stylish capital of Palma, a scattering of Talayotic ruins and ancient sites, as well as Moorish gardens, sleepy villages and serene monasteries. With Eyewitness Top 10 Mallorca, it's yours to explore.

Mallorca's varied landscape makes the island ideal for all kinds of outdoor activities, from hiking and biking in the mountains, to sailing, diving and snorkelling along the coast. There are resorts to suit all visitors, whether you're looking for somewhere relaxed, such as **Port de Pollença**, or want to stay in style at glamorous **Cala Major**.

Mallorca's excellent local cuisine is enjoying a renaissance, reflected in the popularity of its time-honoured traditional eateries, as well as the slew of stellar award-winning restaurants and wineries that are popping up across the island.

Culturally, too, the island packs a remarkable punch: festivals of art, literature and music are held throughout the year, and there are numerous superb museums such as **Es Baluard**, the **Fundació Miró Mallorca** and the **Fundación Yannick y Ben Jakober**. Mallorca is also a fabulous family destination, with plenty to keep the kids amused, from beaches and waterparks to castles, coves and caves.

Whether you're visiting for a weekend or a week, our Top 10 guide brings together the best of everything that Mallorca has to offer, from centuries-old **villages** to marvelous **churches**. The guide has useful tips throughout, from seeking out what's free to avoiding the crowds, plus seven easy-to-follow itineraries designed to tie together a clutch of sights in a short space of time. Add inspiring photography and detailed maps, and you've got the essential pocket-sized travel companion. **Enjoy the book, and enjoy Mallorca.**

Clockwise from top: **Hilltop village of Deià, detail of La Seu in Palma, Cala Figuera harbour, view of Cala Tuent, beach at Port d'Alcúdia, gardens at Raixa, Coves d'es Hams**

Exploring Mallorca

Mallorca's varied coastline boasts everything from hedonistic resorts to secret coves, while the tranquil interior offers stunning mountains, timeless villages and glorious landscapes. To help make the most of your stay, here are ideas for a two-day and a seven-day jaunt around the island.

Magnificent La Seu in Palma is surrounded by elegant and colourful gardens.

Two Days in Mallorca

Day **❶**
MORNING

Spend the morning in Palma, visiting **La Seu** *(see pp12–13)*, and admiring the Modernista buildings *(see pp50–51)*. Then jump on a bus to visit the fairy-tale **Castell de Bellver** *(see pp16–17)*, which offers stunning views over Palma Bay. Stroll downhill for lunch along the seafront.

AFTERNOON

Grab a taxi (or make the 45-minute stroll) to reach the **Fundació Miró Mallorca** *(see pp18–19)*, the striking art centre created at Miró's former home and studio. Head back into town for a fresh seafood dinner.

Day **❷**
MORNING

Take the historic train from Palma to the **Sóller Valley** *(see pp28–9)*, soaking up the impressive views of the Serra de Tramuntana. Spend the morning exploring delightful **Sóller** *(see p101)*.

Key
— Two-day itinerary
— Seven-day itinerary

AFTERNOON

An old tram rattles along from **Sóller** *(see p101)* through orange groves to the **Port de Sóller** *(see p100)*, where you can soak up the rays on the beach, or wander along the coastal path, before heading back to Palma.

Seven Days in Mallorca

Day **❶**

Follow day one of the two-day Mallorca itinerary.

Day **❷**

Take the scenic drive out to **La Granja** *(see pp20–21)* and explore the historic country estate. Stop at **Valldemossa** *(see pp22–3)* for lunch and to visit the monastery, then drive on to enchanting **Deià** *(see pp102–3)* and its picturesque cove *(see p61)*. Dine by the bay in **Port de Sóller** *(see p100)*.

Parc Natural de S'Albufera
has some beautiful beaches.

Day ❺
The next stop is the handsome walled town of **Alcúdia** *(see pp34–5)* and wetlands of the **Parc Natural de S'Albufera** *(see p110)*, located just south of town; both are perfect for hiking and bird-watching.

Day ❻
Devote the morning to **Artà** *(see p122)* and its fascinating Talayotic village at **Ses Païsses** *(see p119)*. Tour the **Coves del Drac** *(see pp36–7)*, the most spectacular of Mallorca's many cave systems, and spend the evening in **Portocolom** *(see p122)*.

Day ❼
Stroll around the country towns of **Felanitx** *(see p122)* and **Santanyí** *(see p122)*, and spend the afternoon on **Es Trenc** *(see p61)*, a glorious 2-km (3-mile) stretch of golden sand. In the evening, return to Palma.

Day ❸
Grab some picnic supplies and head to the **Cala Tuent** *(see p112)* for lunch. Spend the afternoon at the **Monestir de Nostra Senyora de Lluc** *(see pp30–31)*; be sure to catch the boys' choir, Els Blauets, who sing at 1:15pm from Monday to Friday, and at 11pm on Sunday. Arrive in **Pollença** *(see pp110–11)* in time for a drink and supper.

Day ❹
Explore the delightful historic centre of **Pollença**, and spend the afternoon on the spectacular **Península de Formentor** *(see pp32–3)*, perhaps going for a hike up to the watch-tower, or soaking up the sunshine on the wild beach. Return to **Port de Pollença** *(see p110)* for dinner.

The pretty town of Deià is perched on top of a hill, close to the coast.

Top 10 Mallorca Highlights

Sandy Palma beach with the imposing La Seu cathedral in the background

🔟 Mallorca Highlights

Mallorca is laden with history and sights, from its castles and enchanted gardens to caves and spectacular mountains. The eastern and southern coasts still sport some of the cleanest, most beautiful beaches in the Mediterranean, and the city of Palma is more attractive, culturally alive and fun than ever.

La Seu: Palma Cathedral ①

Looming over Palma Bay, this Gothic edifice is as immense as it is pretty. Among the treasures within are the tombs of the island's first kings *(see pp12–15)*.

② Castell de Bellver

Standing sentinel on a hilltop, the castle of Bellver is immaculately preserved. Its walls have imprisoned queens and scholars, and they now contain an intriguing museum that brings to life the island's fascinating past *(see pp16–17)*.

Fundació Miró Mallorca ③

The genius and visionary power of the consummate Catalan artist are demonstrated here. Not only can you experience the full range of Miró's work, but you can also immerse yourself in the atmosphere of his studio *(see pp18–19)*.

④ La Granja

A mountain estate of elegant architecture and bucolic surroundings, this tranquil spot is also home to workshops that once served noble landowners *(see pp20–21)*.

Valldemossa ⑤

One of Mallorca's most beautiful towns, this is where composer Frédéric Chopin and his lover, the writer George Sand, spent a winter in 1838–9 *(see pp22–5)*.

6 Sóller Valley

Surrounded by mountains and beaches, Sóller is referred to as the Golden Valley for its orange and lemon groves *(see pp28–9)*.

7 Monestir de Nostra Senyora de Lluc

Mallorca's most ancient holy site is also its spiritual epicentre. The monastery houses a sacred statue of the Virgin and a small museum *(see pp30–31)*.

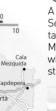

8 Península de Formentor

A dramatic extension of the Serra de Tramuntana mountain range, this is the site of Mallorca's first luxury resort, where kings and movie stars still come to play *(see pp32–3)*.

9 Alcúdia

The island's only remaining medieval walled city, Alcúdia was built on the site of a Roman outpost, the theatre and ruins of which can still be seen *(see pp34–5)*.

10 Coves del Drac

The island's biggest and best caves echo with classical music, played from boats on one of Europe's largest underground lakes *(see pp36–7)*.

🔟 ⭐ La Seu: Palma Cathedral

Palma's cathedral is an imposing pile, with its lofty Gothic buttresses, finials and bosses. Legend has it that King Jaume I ordered its construction after a vow he made to God in 1230, though he merely modified an existing mosque. Work began in 1306 and continues to this day. The west façade was rebuilt after an earthquake in 1851, and controversial touches were added in the 20th century by Gaudí.

1 Exterior
From afar, La Seu **(below)** seems to have more in common with a craggy mountain than it does with any European cathedral. The design depicts the might of the Christian conquerors.

3 Gaudí Modifications
In 1904–14, the great Modernista architect set about improving La Seu's interior, removing mediocre altars and installing electric lights. The controversial baldachin **(right)** is actually only a mock-up – he was never able to finish the final canopy.

2 Bell Tower
The cathedral's enormous bell is set within a late medieval three-storey-high tower surmounted by a "crown of lace" – a perforated stone parapet with small pinnacles.

4 Chapels
The aisles to either side of the nave are flanked by a series of chapels. The highlight is the Capella del Corpus Christi, just to the left of the high altar and with a lovely carved altarpiece.

5 Museum
The collection includes some of La Seu's earliest altar panels, a polychrome wood sarcophagus, ornate reliquaries and furniture. But it is the collection of Mallorcan Primitive paintings that really steal the show.

6 Portal Major
Although it is Gothic in overall style, the main door is the product of Renaissance workmanship. A figure of Mary is surrounded by objects symbolizing her purity.

NEED TO KNOW

MAP M5 ■ Plaça de la Seu, Palma ■ 902 022445 ■ www.catedraldemallorca.org/en

Open Apr–May & Oct: 10am–5:15pm Mon–Fri, 10am–2:15pm Sat; Jun–Sep: 10am–6:15pm Mon–Fri, 10am–2:15pm Sat; Nov–Mar: 10am–3:15pm, 10am–2:15pm Sat

Adm €6

Palau de l'Almudaina: C/Palau Reial, s/n; 902 0444 54; open Oct–Mar: 10am–6pm Tue–Sun; Apr–Sep: 10am–8pm Tue–Sun; adm €7 (call for free entry times); www.patrimonionacional.es

■ From May to October, you can visit the terraces, to admire the stunning views of the harbour. Book ahead (adm €12).

■ Tourist visits are not permitted during Mass.

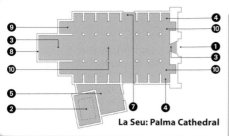

La Seu: Palma Cathedral

GAUDÍ'S SOUNDING BOARD

Antoni Gaudí created an ingenious sounding board to ensure that the priest's voice would be projected throughout the immense cathedral. The wood-and-fabric creation sat above a pulpit until 1972, when new technologies rendered it obsolete and it was removed.

9 Capella del Santíssim

Designed by renowned contemporary Mallorcan artist Miquel Barceló, the Chapel of the Most Holy boasts a large ceramic mural and fine stained-glass windows. The mural is based on the miracle of the Feeding of the Five Thousand, with its images of teeming fish and rustic loaves.

7 Portal del Mirador

The seaward, Gothic façade is the most spectacular side. Ornate buttresses surround an elaborate door **(left)**. It was formerly called the Door of the Apostles but is now known as the Mirador (vantage point).

8 Rose Windows

A vibrant rose window at the end of the nave is the main one of seven (a few are blocked up). Some say the 20th-century "restoration" of the window's coloured glass was too strong.

10 Nave Columns

La Seu is one of Europe's tallest Gothic structures, and the sense of space in its interior is enhanced by graceful, elongated pillars **(above)** that melt away in the upper reaches of the nave.

Palau de l'Almudaina

Key to Floorplan
- Ground floor
- First floor

Palau de l'Almudaina

1 Function of the Palace

Standing directly opposite La Seu, in an equally prominent position that actually obscures the cathedral's main façade from all but close-up view, this ancient royal palace adds a lighter, more graceful note to Palma's assemblage of civic buildings. Today, the palace is mainly used for legislative and military headquarters, but the Royal Family sometimes host ceremonies and state receptions here in the summer.

2 Building Style

An amalgam of Gothic and Moorish styles (the building was once an Islamic fort), the palace has a unique charm. Medieval towers have been topped with dainty Moorish-inspired crenellations. Refined windows and open, airy arcades also tell of an abiding Islamic influence.

3 Hall of Councils

The largest room on the ground floor takes its name, Salón de Consejos, from a meeting of ministers called here in 1983 by Juan Carlos I. There are 16th- and 17th-century Flemish tapestries, coats of arms and furniture.

4 Officers' Mess

The walls of this room are graced with beautiful 17th-century Flemish tapestries and genre paintings, some by a talented contemporary of Rubens.

5 Terrace and Banys Àrabs

Step onto the terrace for spectacular panoramic views. Then, back inside, peer into the remains of the Arab Baths. By means of mirrors, visitors can examine the three separate vaulted chambers below – one for hot, one for tepid and one for cold water.

6 Chapel of St Anne

This chapel's impressive, delicately coloured altarpiece, created in Barcelona in 1358, is a visual sonnet in sky blue and gold.

Interior of the Chapel of St Anne

7 Central Courtyard

Known variously as the Patio de Armas, the Patio de Honor and the Patio del Castillo, this central courtyard also evokes Moorish architecture, with its elegantly looping arches and central stand of palm trees. A small fountain incorporates a 10th-century lion sculpture from the original Islamic fort.

8 Queen's Office

The Royal Staircase to the upper floor leads to the Queen's Office, which contains fine antiques, tapestries and paintings.

9 King's Rooms

Decorations in these rooms include huge 17th-century Flemish tapestries, bronze statuary, and Neo-Classical paintings, as well as some spectacular Empire furniture with glittering ormolu adornments.

10 Gothic Hall

This remarkable room, noted for its huge pointed arches, is used to hold official receptions. Try not to miss the fine 16th-century Flemish tapestry (on the back wall), which depicts the Siege of Carthage.

MALLORCA'S UNIQUE ARCHITECTURAL HERITAGE

Mallorca has a good supply of quality stone and much of it has been easy to quarry. There's also a ready supply of timber among the forests of the Serra de Tramuntana. The prehistoric Talayotic peoples used stone for their villages – Ses Païsses near Artà *(see p122)* is a prime example. The Romans also favoured stone buildings, as in the ruins of Pollentia on the edge of Alcúdia *(see p35)*. The Moors, who governed the island from the early 8th to the 13th century, specialized in ornate timber decoration. The best surviving example of this Mudéjar architectural style is at the Jardins de Alfàbia *(see p63)*. After the Christian reconquest of Mallorca in 1229, Jaume I and his successors used stone for all their key structures, including religious buildings, the most beautiful of which is La Seu *(see pp12–13)*. In the early 20th century, wealthier Mallorcans favoured the Spanish version of Art Nouveau – Modernista – a style adopted in several buildings in both Palma *(see pp50–51)* and Sóller *(see pp28–9)*.

TOP 10
TYPICAL FEATURES OF TRADITIONAL HOUSES

1 Kitchen fireplace

2 *Clastra* (main patio)

3 Cisterns

4 *Tafona* (oil press) and mill room

5 Defence tower

6 *Capilla* (family chapel)

7 Stone walls, floors and sometimes ceilings

8 Vaulted ceilings

9 Wood beams

10 Motifs derived from Islamic, Gothic, Rococo, Italian Renaissance, Baroque, Neo-Classical or Modernista styles

Stone exterior of the Palau de l'Almudaina showing Moorish influences

TOP 10 ⭐ Castell de Bellver

Among the world's most striking castles, Castell de Bellver – located near Palma – was a grand 14th-century royal fortress, a royal summer residence and later a royal prison. It now houses a small museum on the history of Palma. Surrounded for miles by fragrant pine woods, the castle has stunning views over Palma Bay (*bellver* means "lovely view" in Catalan). It is hard to believe that this perfectly preserved building has been standing for 700 years.

1 Views
Go to the top for 360-degree views, including the foothills and sea to the west and the mountains to the north. The perfume of the pine forests creates a heady mix with the sea breezes.

Central Courtyard 2
The two-tiered central courtyard **(right)** has 21 Catalan Romanesque arches on the lower tier and 42 octagonal columns supporting 21 Gothic arches on the upper tier. Statues of Venus and Nero grace the walkway.

3 Defence Towers
The castle has three horseshoe-shaped towers **(left)** and four smaller protuberances that were used for guard posts. Their windows have narrow slits, so that archers could attack without fear of being hit by the enemy.

NEED TO KNOW

MAP C4 ■ 3 km (2 miles) W of the city centre ■ 971 735065

Open Apr–Sep: 10am–7pm Tue–Sat (until 3pm Sun & hols); Oct–Mar: 10am–6pm Tue–Sat (until 3pm Sun & hols)

Adm €4 (free for under-14s; Sun)

■ You can reach the Bellver hill by car or taxi, or take city bus 50, which stops at the castle. Bus 46 will take you to Plaça Gomila. To reach the castle from here, climb through the woods above Carrer de Bellver.

■ For a good-value Mediterranean lunch, stop at the Hostal Corona (C/Josep Villalonga, 22; 971 731935) and enjoy a meal in their lovely garden patio.

4 Castle Ditch
In case the castle's thick walls and projecting turrets were insufficient deterrents for would-be attackers, Mallorcan kings also surrounded the castle with an earthen ditch. The drawbridge would be lifted in the event of a siege.

6 Museum: Ground Floor
A museum on the history of Palma surrounds the central courtyard. Displays and exhibits on the ground floor level trace the story of the city from its Roman beginnings in 123 BC to the present day.

Castell de Bellver

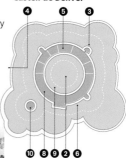

Key to Floorplan
- Ground floor
- First floor

9 Prison
Until 1915, the lower reaches of this castle were used as a prison, dubbed La Olla (the pot). Jaume III's widow and sons (see p41) were imprisoned here for most of their lives.

10 Keep Tower
The free-standing castle keep, called the Torre de Homenaje **(below)**, is almost twice as high as the castle itself, and is connected to its roof by a small bridge supported by a slim, pointed Gothic archway. It is only open to visitors by advance arrangement.

5 Museum: First Floor
The first floor of the museum displays a wide range of Roman statues, busts and effigies **(below)** that were collected by 18th-century antiquarian Cardinal Antonio Despuig. They were originally on show at Raixa (see p102).

7 Circular Design
The round shape of the main structure is unique among Spanish castles and a fine example of 14th-century military architecture. The circular structure also aided in the collection of rainwater into the central cistern.

8 Hermaphroditus
The museum's star exhibit is an alabaster statue of the Greek god Hermaphroditus, whose body merged with that of a nymph when he rejected her advances. He is having a troubled night's sleep, hence the dishevelled appearance.

TOP 10 ⭐ Fundació Miró Mallorca

The artist Joan Miró lived and worked in Cala Major from 1956 until his death in 1983. His house and studios were bequeathed to the public and converted into an art centre. The Fundació headquarters' modern edifice is the work of Rafael Moneo, a leading Spanish architect. It offers an insight into Miró's creative process through changing exhibitions from the museum's extensive collection of his paintings, drawings and sculptures, as well as works by international artists.

1 Works on Canvas

Many of these works from the 1960s and 1970s are made with mixed media – oil, chalk, acrylic and pastel. Some may have been inspired by Japanese Zen action painting. Some pieces are blue **(left)** – for Miró, this was the most universal and optimistic colour – while others are in black and white.

2 Temporary Exhibitions

The temporary exhibition spaces feature the works of international artists and cover some of the lesser-known aspects of Miró's work.

3 Works on Paper

On display are several works on paper, most exhibiting the signature primary colours and bright splashes for which the artist is known.

4 Garden

In the garden, groups of rocks resembling water lilies "float" in a pool, while in other niches works by avant-garde and modern artists can be found.

5 Sculptures

Various vaguely anthropomorphic sculptures **(left)**, greet visitors in the garden, which functions as a gallery in itself. Downstairs, the giant *Woman and Bird* was made with ceramicist Llorenç Artigast.

6 Son Boter

This 18th-century estate was Miró's second studio. Workshops and courses by international artists are held at the nearby centre.

NEED TO KNOW

MAP C4 ■ C/Joan de Saridakis, 29, Palma ■ 971 701420 ■ www.miromallorca.com

Open mid-May–mid-Sep: 10am–7pm Tue–Sat, 10am–3pm Sun & hols; mid-Sep–mid-May: 10am–6pm Tue–Sat; 10am–3pm Sun & hols

Adm €7.50 (call for free times)

■ Bus (EMT 3, 20 and 46), taxi or driving are good ways to get to the centre.

■ An enlightening film on Miró is shown during the day (in five different languages).

■ The excellent café serves sandwiches, *pa amb oli (see p76)*, olives, fresh orange juice and more. It features a wonderful mural by Miró and there is no entry fee for the public.

7 Taller Sert Studio

Miró's studio **(below)** looks like the artist just stepped out for a break from work in progress. Objects that inspired Miró are all around: Hopi *kachina* dolls, a bat skeleton, Mexican terracottas and other everyday items.

8 Murals

Above one of the garden pools, a black rectangle encloses a ceramic mural by Miró, with colourful shapes gyrating in space. Taking up a whole wall in the café is a large mural of the sun and other celestial bodies.

MIRÓ'S STYLE

Joan Miró (1893–1983), one of the best-known artists of the 20th century, was a Catalan through and through. Initially influenced by Fauvism, and later by Dadaism and Surrealism, he developed his own unique style, marked by lyricism and lively colouring. After arriving in Mallorca he became interested in graphics, ceramics and sculpture, scoring significant successes in every art form. The embodiment of a uniquely Catalan way of seeing the world, he became one of the greatest exponents of Surrealism.

10 Mural del Sol

Usually on display is this five-panel sketch on paper, which formed the study for a mural commissioned for the UNESCO building in Paris, co-created with Llorenç Artigas in 1955–8. The work won the Guggenheim award.

Fundació Miró Mallorca

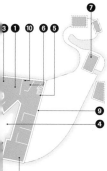

9 Building Design

Composed of concrete made to look like travertine marble, the starkly modern building **(below)** is softened by reflecting pools and trees. Its narrow windows afford surprising views from the hilltop site. Huge refined alabaster panels are also used as translucent walls, softly lighting exhibition spaces.

TOP 10 ⭐ La Granja

This *possessió* (country estate) is on a site known since Roman times for its natural spring. In 1239, Count Nuño Sanz donated the estate to Cistercian monks; since 1447 it has been a private house. Visitors come today mainly to see rural Mallorcan traditions, such as demonstrations of lace-making, embroidery and spinning, and for tastings of cheese, wine, sausages, doughnuts and fig cake.

Loggia ①
The loveliest architectural feature of the house evokes Florentine tenets of beauty and grace with considerable success. Providing a welcome breezeway on hot summer days and charming vistas at any time of the year, this elegant gallery **(right)**, unusual in Mallorca, is a place at which to pause.

② Forecourt
The majestic space in front of the mansion contains four large plane trees that are about 150 years old. Here visitors can relax in their shade, watching craftsmen at work and sampling regional wines, liqueurs, juices, jams, *sobrassadas* (sausages), cheeses, figs, breads and *bunyolas* (potato flour buns).

③ Shows
Handicraft shows and horse and falconry displays are staged on Wednesdays and Fridays.

④ Workrooms
The labyrinth of rooms downstairs comprises the earthy heart of the home **(below)**. The estate was self-sufficient with its own tinsmith, oil-mill, winepress, distilleries (for liqueurs and cosmetics), woodworking shop and more.

⑤ Family Apartments
These rooms evoke a genteel country lifestyle. Of particular note are the curtains in the main room made of *roba de llengües*; the study with its medical instruments; and the antique toys in the games room.

⑥ Cellars
Cheeses were manufactured in the cellars, using the milk of cows, sheep and goats. Flour was ground with a stone mill to make all types of pasta. Dairy products, oil, wine and grain were all stored here.

8 Chapel

The altarpiece, with its lovely festooned arch, is Baroque; the altar itself is a pretty Gothic creation; and the two kneeling, silver-winged plaster angels **(left)** are rather kitsch 19th-century designs.

9 Dining Room

The main attraction here is the cleverly constructed dining-room table **(below)** that doubles as a billiard table. The crockery and glassware, from various eras, are original to the house, and the tile floor is also original.

TRADITIONAL MUSIC AND DANCING

Fashioned from wood and animal skins, Mallorcan instruments include the *xeremia* (bagpipe), *fabiol* (flute), *tamborino* and *guitarro*. Typical famous dances are the Bolero (18th century), La Jota (from eastern Mallorca), the Fandango (a line dance), Copeo and Mateixa (both also from the east). Many informal dances are improvised, accompanied only by percussion; an organized ensemble will perform on formal occasions.

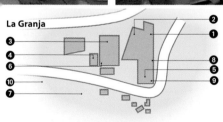

La Granja

7 Gardens

The cultivated areas offer lots to see, including a walled rock garden, a pond with a water-jet fountain, moss-covered rock formations, botanical gardens and a magnificent 1,000-year-old yew tree. The stream that was used for irrigation can still be seen.

10 Waterfalls and Woods

With surprising speed, you can leave the delights of La Granja behind for a walk in the thick, surrounding woodlands. The scenery is spectacular, and one of the walking trails leads to something of an island rarity – a waterfall.

NEED TO KNOW

MAP B3 ■ Ctra Esporles-Banyalbufar, km 2, Esporles (follow signs off the main coast road, MA-1100) ■ 971 610032 ■ www.lagranja.net

Open 10am–7pm daily (Nov–Mar: until 6pm)

Adm €15.50 adults; €9 children (4–12 years)

■ The easiest way to get to La Granja is by car or tour bus.

■ The Granja Restaurant serves lunch all day. Picnics can be had within the grounds.

Valldemossa

This small, picturesque town in the mountains is arguably where Mallorcan tourism began one cold winter in 1838, when composer Frédéric Chopin and his lover, the female writer George Sand, rented some rooms at the former monastery here. Shunned by locals, the couple had a miserable time, as portrayed in Sand's book *A Winter in Majorca*. However, Mallorcans today are proud of their Chopin–Sand connection, and the book is sold everywhere.

1 Old Town
The old town (below) spills down a hillside, surrounded by farmed terraces and *marjades* (stone walls) created 1,000 years ago by the Moors. The name "Valldemossa" comes from the original land-owner, Muza. Visit the charming shops here, including those that sell artisan goods.

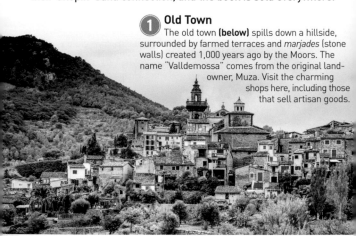

NEED TO KNOW

MAP C3

Monastery Cells (2 and 4): open Apr–Oct: 10am–6pm Mon–Sat (until 2pm Sun); Jul & Aug: 10am–6:30pm Mon–Sat (until 2pm Sun)

Monastery Complex: open Nov–Mar: 10am–4:30pm Mon–Sat; Dec & Jan: 10am–3:30pm Mon–Sat; adm €9.50 adults, €4 children (10–14 years, under-10s free)

Museu Municipal de Valldemossa: 971 612106; open 10am–4:30pm Mon–Sat

■ If you drive in, park in a municipal car park, then explore on foot.

2 Monastery: Cells 2 and 4
Said to be the rooms that Chopin and Sand rented, the cells are full of memorabilia, including Chopin's piano, Sand's manuscripts, busts (right) and portraits.

3 Monastery Complex
The town's top attraction is the former monastery where Chopin and Sand stayed, now home to a palace and a municipal museum *(see pp24–5)*. Given to the Carthusian Order in 1399, the estate was a monastery until 1835, when religious orders were ousted from the island. It was bought by a banker, who rented the rooms to Chopin.

4 Monastery: Pharmacy
Laden with tinctures and various exotic elixirs, a deconsecrated chapel faithfully re-creates the estate's original pharmacy. George Sand bought marshmallow here in a futile attempt to cure Chopin's unremitting tuberculosis.

Valldemossa

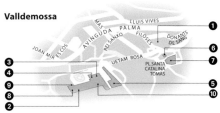

6 Birthplace of Santa Catalina Thomás

Mallorca's only saint, Catalina Thomás (known as the "Beatata" for both her diminutive stature and saintliness), was born at a house on C/Rectoría, 5 in 1531. The house was converted into an oratory in 1792 and features saintly scenes **(left)** and a statue of her holding a bird. She was finally canonized in 1930 and many locals honour her with plaques by their doors.

7 Church of Sant Bartomeu

Near the bottom of the old town, a rustic, Baroque-style church is dedicated to one of the patron saints of the town. It was erected in 1245, shortly after Jaume I conquered Mallorca, and extended in the early 18th century. The bell tower and façade were added after 1863.

5 Monastery: Palace

The monastery's core was once the site of the palace built by Jaume II for his son **(below)**. The rooms are regally decorated – a beautiful piece is the 12th-century woodcarving of Madonna and Child. Concerts of Chopin's music are also held here.

8 Monastery: Prior's Cell

The head of the monks had a private oratory, a magnificent library, an elegant audience chamber, a bedroom, a dining room, an Ave María (praying alcove) and, of course, a sumptuous garden.

9 Monastery: Church

The Neo-Classical church has a cupola adorned with frescoes **(above)** by Fray Manuel Bayeu, Francisco de Goya's brother-in-law. It is distinguished by barrel vaulting and gilt-edged stucco work.

10 Monastery: Cloisters

From the church, visitors can enter the cloisters known as the Myrtle Court. Around it are six chapels and ten spacious monks' cells. The International Chopin Festival is held here annually.

Museu Municipal de Valldemossa

Pretty courtyard at the Museu Municipal de Valldemossa

① Archduke Luis Salvador of Habsburg-Lorena and Bourbon

On the ground floor here is a room dedicated to Archduke Luis Salvador, an indefatigable chronicler of Mediterranean life, whose absolute passion was Mallorcan culture. His nine volumes on the Balearics are the most exhaustive study ever made of the archipelago.

② Guasp Printworks

On the ground floor of the museum visitors will also find a 17th-century hand press and one of the finest collections of 1,584 intricate boxwood engravings in

The working Guasp printing press

Europe. On the walls are prints executed on the press, which is still in working order.

③ Mallorcan Painters of the Tramuntana

Mallorca's mountainous Tramuntana region has long attracted the skills of landscape painters. Among the outstanding artists shown are Bartomeu Ferrà, Joan Fuster and Antoni Ribas.

④ Catalan and Spanish Painters of the Tramuntana

Works by Sebastià Junyer, and more Impressionistic pieces by Eliseo Meifrén, are displayed here.

⑤ International Painters of the Tramuntana

These include the 21st-century Italian master Aligi Sassu, whose works owe much to Futurism, Surrealism and Expressionism.

⑥ Contemporary Art: Juli Ramis

The contemporary collection was conceived as a spotlight on Juli Ramis (1909–90), one of the most important 20th-century Mallorcan painters. Works on display include his signature *Dama Blava* and pieces by his Paris contemporaries, showing a cross-fertilization of influences.

7 Miró

Of note is *El Vol de l'Alosa* (Flight of the Swallows) – Miró's whimsical illustrations for the works of Mallorcan poets in his signature bold and colourful style.

8 Picasso

Pablo Picasso, a lifelong friend of Miró and a frequent visitor to the area, is also represented in the museum's collection. There are several of his paintings of bulls and bullfighters, as well as some fine examples of book illustrations.

9 Tàpies

Also in the last room are a few works by another great Catalan painter, Antoni Tàpies. Master of an elegant and totally unique artistic style, he created works that have little in common with the more Surrealist images of his compatriots Miró and Dalí, and are considerably more understated, poetic and monumental.

10 Other 20th-Century Artists

Finally, there is a collection of some small but significant engravings and lithographs by great modern artists from around the world, including German Surrealist Max Ernst, Italian Futurist Robert Matta, French Dadaist André Masson, the English master Henry Moore and British-Irish painter Francis Bacon.

FROM MASS TOURISM TO CULTURE AND ECOLOGY

Black vulture

Once an isolated backwater, Mallorca became known for all the wrong reasons after Sand's account of her disastrous trip with Chopin in *A Winter in Majorca*. By the early 20th century, however, Jules Verne was imagining its caves and the Kaiser was cruising its waters. In the 1960s, the island turned its attention to mass tourism with rapid development that resulted in scores of high-rise hotels. Since the early 21st century, greater emphasis has been placed on culture and ecology. Nature parks have been created, salt pans saved, the black vulture spared from extinction, and inland and rural buildings have been protected as part of the island's heritage.

TOP 10 CULTURAL AND ECOLOGICAL ATTRACTIONS

1 Balearic public nature parks S'Albufera, Mondragó, Sa Dragonera, S'Albufera Nature Reserve, Serra de Llevant

2 Cabrera National Park

3 Agrotourism

4 Rural hotels

5 Centres for traditional culture La Granja, Els Calderers, Jardins de Alfàbia, Raixa, Gordiola Glassworks

6 Archaeological and historical museums

7 Accommodation in monasteries

8 Mountain shelters

9 Animal rescue and endangered species programmes

10 UNESCO World Heritage Site Serra de Tramuntana

Lily pond at the Jardí Botànic de Sóller

Following pages Altar in the Basilica at the Monestir de Nostra Senyora de Lluc

🔟 ⭐ Sóller Valley

Famous for its orange and lemon groves, Sóller, an enchanting town embraced by the Tramuntana mountains on the northwest coast, is often referred to as the heart of the Golden Valley. During the late 19th and early 20th centuries, many locals traded oranges, olive oil and textiles with France through Sóller's bustling port. The picturesque neighbouring villages of Fornalutx and Biniaraix can be reached on foot from the Plaça de Constitució.

① Historic Train and Tram

The historic train travels through pretty mountain scenery on its hour-long journey from Palma to Sóller. A vintage tram **(below)** trundles through orange groves between Sóller and the port.

② Jardins de Alfàbia

A legacy of the Moorish talent for landscaping and irrigation, these gardens *(see p42)* date back to the 13th century. As well as providing a fabulous oasis for visitors, Alfàbia is a working farm.

③ Can Prunera Art Museum

Set in an Art Nouveau building, with period furniture and fittings **(right)**, this museum exhibits work by 19th- and 20th-century artists such as Picasso and Miró.

④ Balearic Museum of Natural Sciences

This museum inside an old palace holds a great collection dedicated to the study of nature and conservation in the Balearic Islands. See the library and classroom, and the botanical gardens nearby.

⑤ Fet a Sóller

Head to Fet a Sóller, by the market square, where authentic ice cream is made, and choose from 40 delicious flavours and sorbets made from natural ingredients. There is also a café and a small gift shop for souvenirs.

Sóller Valley

5 km (3 miles)

9 Biniaraix Village

This village *(see p104)* comes alive in the holiday season and on weekends, when walkers flock to its cobbled Barranc steps. These lead to the Cuber reservoir and L'Ofre, one of the Tramuntanas' highest peaks.

8 Cap de Gros Lighthouse

It is worth the steep walk up the mountain road to the landmark Cap de Gros lighthouse above Sóller port. Although it was built in 1842, it was not fitted with electricity until 1918. The views out to sea and across the bay are magnificent.

10 Plaça de Constitució

Sóller's main square **(above)** is ideal for people-watching. Directly on the *plaça* stands the sandstone church of Sant Bartomeu, parts of which date from the 1100s. Nearby is the pretty Art Nouveau Bank of Sóller, built in 1912.

6 Port de Sóller

The picturesque port area **(above)** offers many restaurants, sandy beaches and fabulous views *(see p57)*. A steep walk up leads to Oratorio de Santa Caterina, built in 1280. The Jumeirah Luxury Spa & Hotel is also worth a visit.

7 Fornalutx Village

This labyrinthine village in the Tramuntanas is a pleasant walk from the main square. This traditional settlement *(see p54)* has stunning mountain views, a small plaça (square) and a 17th-century church.

NEED TO KNOW
MAP C2

Balearic Museum of Natural Sciences: Palma–Port Sóller road, km 30; 971 634064; open Apr–Oct: 10am–6pm Mon–Sat, Nov–Mar: 10am–2pm Tue–Sat; adm €8; www.museuciencies naturals.org

Can Prunera Art Museum: 971 638973; open Mar–Oct: 10:30am–6pm daily, Nov–Mar: 10:30am–6:30pm Tue–Sun; adm €5; www.canprunera.com

Jardins de Alfàbia: Ctra de Sóller, km 17, Bunyola; 971 613123; open Mar: 9:30am–5:30pm Mon–Fri (until 1:30pm Sat), Apr–Oct: 9:30am–6:30pm daily; adm €7.50; www.jardines dealfabia.com

Fet a Sóller: Plaça des Mercat; 971 635179; open 10am–8pm daily; www. fetasoller.com

■ The garden snack bar at Jardins de Alfàbia offers fresh juices, nuts, fruits and snacks, all produced at its working farm.

🔟⭐ Monestir de Nostra Senyora de Lluc

The monastery at Lluc is the spiritual centre of Mallorca and has been a place of pilgrimage for over 800 years. The main point of interest is the little statue of the Virgin (La Moreneta). The story goes that it was found by a local shepherd boy who showed it to the nearest monk. The image was initially moved to the church but it kept returning to the same spot, so a chapel was built to house it. Each year, thousands of pilgrims come to pay homage.

3 La Moreneta
In a special chapel **(left)** stands the object of pilgrimage, La Moreneta ("the Little Dark One") – or, to be more precise, a mid-13th-century, possibly Flemish, version of her. Unfortunately, the 1960s lighting detracts from the atmosphere.

4 Museum: Religious Artifacts
Pieces on display include a Byzantine *trikerion* (three-part sacred utensil), a 15th-century wooden tabernacle, a 15th-century Flemish Virgin and Child, a gold filigree reliquary for a Piece of the True Cross and devotional paintings.

1 The Complex
The complex is rather plain but is set in fragrant forests of pine and holm oak, and laid out around courtyards. There is a good hostel, a choir school, several eateries, campsites, picnic facilities and a covered area for outdoor celebrations and services.

2 El Camí dels Misteris del Rosari
"The Way of the Mysteries of the Rosary" is a pilgrim route up the hillside behind the complex, where a crucifix awaits. The path is punctuated by bronze sculptures framed in stone.

5 Basilica Entrance
Facing an inner courtyard, the church's façade is an appealing Baroque confection that relieves the plainness of the surrounding structures **(below)**. The bronze statue here is that of a bishop who helped to renovate the place in the early 1900s.

Monestir de Nostra Senyora de Lluc

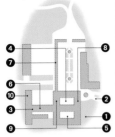

8 Museum: Majolica

In the 15th century, Italy imported large amounts of tin-glazed pottery from Spain by way of the trade route through Mallorca, hence the term "majolica", from the medieval name of the island. Until the early 20th century, this type of pottery was also produced in Mallorca.

NEED TO KNOW

MAP E2 ■ Plaza Peregrins 1, Lluc ■ 971 871525 ■ www.lluc.net

Museu de Lluc: open 10am–2pm Sun–Fri; adm €4

■ Visitors can follow the signposted footpaths to explore the natural surroundings. Check the website to book a stay at the monastery.

■ Head for Sa Fonda, which offers Mallorcan fare (closed in July). Or try the Café Sa Plaça for snacks, or Restaurant Ca S'Amitger *(Plaça Peregrins, 6)* for roast lamb, goat and rice *brut*, a Mallorcan country dish.

9 Museu de Lluc

A broad collection of Mallorcana includes prehistoric and ancient artifacts, coins, religious treasures, vestments, sculptures, ceramics and paintings, as well as model Mallorcan rooms from the 17th century.

6 Basilica Interior

The church **(above)** was deemed a Minor Basilica by the Pope – its embellishments are probably the reason. Crystal chandeliers light the way, and the gold altarpiece is alive with figures.

10 Els Blauets

The 50-boy choir Els Blauets (The Blues) was established in 1531, and is named after their blue cassocks **(below)**. They sing at 1:15pm from Monday to Friday and at 11am on Sunday.

7 Els Porxets

The gallery of the old pilgrim's hospice is a picturesque arcaded corridor, with ground-floor stables and bedrooms off the passageway on the upper level. Declared a Spanish Historical Artistic Monument, it has been carefully restored.

🔟 ⭐ Península de Formentor

The final jutting spur of the Serra de Tramuntana has stunning views, sandy beaches and the island's original luxury resort. With weird rock formations and jagged edges pointing up at 45 degrees, its mountains rise to over 330 m (1,000 ft). The drive from Port de Pollença has dramatic scenery and is known for its tight bends.

4 Lighthouse
Around the last curve, you come upon the silver-domed lighthouse **(below)**, set on a dramatic promontory with views out to sea. On a clear day, you can see all the way to Menorca.

1 Hotel Formentor
This exclusive luxury resort *(see p145)* has been spoiling the rich and famous since 1929. Part of the Platja de Formentor is reserved for hotel guests only.

2 Beach
In a long, sheltered cove with fine sand and clear turquoise water **(above)**, pretty Platja de Formentor is served both by road and a regular ferry from the Port de Pollença. Eating spots and *tiki* shades abound. Expect crowds of families at weekends.

NEED TO KNOW
MAP F1
....
■ To avoid the heaviest traffic, visit early or late in the day. On the way to the watchtower, park at the turn-off just after the first bunkers, slightly down from the top. This will help avoid the parking snarls at the top.

■ The Lighthouse snack bar has nibbles and drinks of all kinds. Sit on the broad terrace for incredible views.

■ For something more refined, as well as far more expensive, head for the five-star Hotel Formentor's beach restaurant Platja Mar *(971 899100)* on the return journey.

3 Cap de Formentor
The terrain becomes rockier towards the end of the peninsula, where the view plunges down to Cala Figuera, Mallorca's most inaccessible beach. It is a challenging drive out to the end, but the breathtaking views **(below)** are rewarding.

9 Peninsula Road

The famous winding coastal road is narrow but well maintained, forking off to the Hotel Formentor in one direction and across to the cape in the other. Side roads along the way – some of which are not well maintained – wind up to the watchtower and give access to the beach, as well as makeshift car parks for Cala Figuera.

5 Talaia d'Albercutx

The watchtower **(above)** has an amazing view over the Peninsula and bays of Pollença and Alcúdia. The road to it is very rough and best tackled with a four-wheel drive. For a further adrenaline rush, hike up the last bit and climb the tower itself.

6 Main Miradors

Of the main miradors (viewpoints), Mirador de Mal Pas is closest to the road. From here it is possible to walk along a wall with dizzying panoramas of the rocks and sea below.

7 Mountain Tunnel

The road continues through pine woods and past more miradors on its way to Es Fumat mountain. It then tunnels through the raw rock of the mountain. For those who need more thrills, there is a steep staircase up the cliff above the tunnel's western mouth.

Península de Formentor

Cap de Catalunya

Cap de Formentor

Los Farollones

Cala Bòquer

Cala Murta

Can es Faro

Illa de Formentor

8 Flora and Fauna

The peninsula is all wild: pine trees mostly, with scrub and clump grasses, oregano, cactus and palmetto everywhere. On a hot summer's day, with cicadas buzzing, walkers will likely see goats, lizards and birds.

10 Casas Velles

An old Mallorcan house is preserved in the grounds of the Hotel Formentor. There is a characteristic courtyard with an old stone well, a one-room house and a small chapel complete with a melodramatic, life-size crucifix.

TOP 10 ⭐ Alcúdia

Located at the base of a peninsula, this delightful walled town was originally a Phoenician settlement and the capital of the island under the Romans. It was later destroyed by the Vandals, then rebuilt by the Moors, and prospered as a trading centre well into the 19th century. Extensively restored, the town contains many historical sites of interest from its fascinating past.

1 Ca'n Torró Library

Opened in 1990, the library (above) is housed in a prime example of 14th-century aristocratic architecture. It hosts concerts and expositions.

2 Oratori de Sant Ana

The tiny medieval chapel, on the main road to Port d'Alcúdia, was built in the 13th century and has a stone carving of a rather stocky Virgin and Child supported by an angel.

3 Teatre Romà

The island's only intact Roman theatre (right) is also Spain's smallest surviving example. Even so, it would have held about 2,000 people, and today is sometimes the venue for special concerts.

4 Ajuntament

The handsome Renaissance-style edifice was given its present look in 1929. Above the balcony is a grand tower with a clock, belfry and weather vane, its over-hanging pitched roofs gaily tiled in red-and-green stripes.

5 Arab Quarter

The narrow streets of the old town are reso-nant of life under Moorish rule, long after Roman orderliness was buried. No one knows where the old *souk* (market) was, but it is easy to imagine artisans' shops spilling onto the dusty streets.

⑥ City Walls

The walls were constructed after the Spanish conquest in the 14th century, with a second ring added in the 17th century. By the 19th century they had begun to show their age and the vagaries of expansion, but they have now been restored almost to their original state. They are adorned with gates and 26 towers in all.

⑧ Historic Centre

While modern Alcúdia extends beyond the old city walls and has a commercial port town attached to it (see p57), most of the sights of historic interest are located within or near the walls. These include churches, mansions, a museum and some of the island's most significant Roman ruins.

⑩ Sant Jaume Church

The 14th-century church collapsed in the winter of 1870 but has since been rebuilt. The rose window is lovely, and the inner recesses feature elaborate gold altars (above). There is also a museum.

⑦ Pollentia Ruins

The Roman city (above) reached its peak in the 1st and 2nd centuries AD, and the foundations of what may have been the forum and insulae (apartments) are visible. Many of the stones have been removed over the years.

⑨ Beaches

From Alcúdia's main beach – the 7-km- (4-mile-) long stretch of the Platja Gran – to the secret coves of the Cap de Pinar, this beautiful stretch of Mallorca's northwestern coastline has a glorious choice of beaches and bays.

Alcúdia

NEED TO KNOW
MAP F2

Ca'n Torró Library: C/d'en Serra, 15; 971 547311; open Oct–May: 10am–2pm Tue–Sun, 5–9pm Tue–Fri; Jun–Sep: 10am–2pm Tue–Sun, 4–8pm Tue–Fri

Teatre Romà: C/de Sant Ana; open access

Sant Jaume Church: Plaça Jaume Quès; 971 548665; open May–Oct: 10am–1pm Mon–Sat; Mass: 8pm Tue–Sun (7:30pm winter), 9:30am, noon Sun; adm €1

■ Visitors arriving by car should find ample parking just outside the old walls.

■ Right in the heart of town, Sa Plaça is popular for its salted fish.

■ There are lots of good places to eat in Port d'Alcúdia. Try the cafés along the waterfront or head to Como en Casa (971 549033), which serves great salads and tapas.

⓽⓪⭐ Coves del Drac

Discovered in ancient times, these limestone caves were first mapped out by French geologist Edouard Martel in 1896. They have since become one of Mallorca's top attractions for both locals and tourists. Hundreds of people at a time make their way along the cavernous path, where artfully lit rock formations and lakes conjure up marvellous imagery. The name "Drac" comes from the Catalan word for "dragon", probably in reference to the mythical creature's role as the fierce guardian of secret treasure.

① Garden
As most visitors will have to wait a little before their tour begins, there is a thoughtfully created garden by the entrance. Mediterranean trees and plants, such as olives, figs, violets and hibiscus, provide the setting for striking displays of limestone – one piece even evokes the shape of a dragon. Gorgeous peacocks roam freely around the gardens, too. Visitors can bring a picnic.

③ Four Chambers
Visitors descend to the caves through the Luis Armand Chamber, part of the Frenchman's Cave, which was discovered by Martel. The three other main caverns are called Black Cave, White Cave and Luis Salvador's Cave. The path is smooth and even, and the guides are temporarily silent, so that visitors have the opportunity to contemplate the beauty of the place.

② Boat Ride
As a delightful climax to the sound-and-light performance, visitors are offered boat rides **(above)** on the lake – eight to a boat – steered by skilled gondoliers who employ an elegant figure-of-eight rowing style.

④ The Snow-Capped Mountain Stalactite
It was Archduke Luis Salvador *(see p24)* who commissioned a team of Frenchmen to investigate the caves. He particularly loved the snow-capped mountain stalactite in the first chamber.

NEED TO KNOW

MAP G4 ■ Porto Cristo ■ 971 820753 ■ www.cuevasdeldrach.com

Open 10am– 5pm daily; Mar–Oct: hourly tours except 1pm, Nov–Feb: tours at 10:45am, noon, 2pm & 3:45pm

Adm €16 adults, €9 children (buy online for reduced rates)

■ An on-site bar/café sells snacks and drinks.

■ Visitors should wear appropriate shoes as the terrain is rough. It can also get cold.

■ Free Wi-Fi, parking and picnic areas available.

7 Lighting
The illuminations in the caves are the work of light engineer Carlos Buigas. Crevices, planes, chasms and spaces are all highlighted in a variety of colours to maximize the effects of chiaroscuro and depth **(left)**. The lighting was installed in 1935.

MALLORCA'S CAVES

The Coves del Drac and the Coves d'es Hams are the best known of Mallorca's cave systems, but there are many more. The stalagmites and stalactites of the Coves de Campanet and the Coves d'Artà (the latter also features a sound-and-light show) are quite impressive, while the Coves de Gènova are conveniently accessible from Palma, if a little less dramatic.

9 Performances
Seated in an amphitheatre, the audience is regaled with a display at the end of the tour. Hypnotic lighting effects accompany live music from a quartet on a rowing boat. High-lights include Albinoni's *Adagio*, Pachelbel's *Canon* and serene works by Chopin, Handel, Boccherini, Bach and others. Photography is not permitted here.

5 Formations
The stalactites (those hanging from above), stalagmites (those below), and columns (where the two meet) range from the finest needles to monumental massifs **(above)**. There are also deep ravines, at the bottom of which are impossibly turquoise pools.

6 Exit
Visitors exit the complex by foot, past the Lake of the Grand Duchess of Tuscany and Chamber of the Columns to the Vestibule, a funnel-like tunnel leading back up to the surface.

8 Fanciful Figures
Formations dubbed the "Inquisition Chamber" or "Ariadne's Labyrinth" were so named in the Middle Ages; the "Snowy Mount" and "Ruined Castle" speak of more modern imaginations.

10 Subterranean Lakes
Lake Martel **(below)** is one of the world's largest, at 177 m (580 ft) long, with an average width of 30 m (98 ft). Its calm waters beautifully reflect the lighting effects of the performances.

The Top 10 of Everything

The historic town of Valldemossa, famous for its Carthusian monastery

🔟 Moments in History

Ruins of a prehistoric town, Montuiri

1 Prehistory

Neolithic pastoral societies have formed by at least 4000 BC. They live in caves and keep domesticated animals. As bronze-working is introduced around 1400 BC, the Talayot period begins and structures such as Ses Païsses *(see p42)* and Capocorb Vell *(see p43)* are constructed.

2 Carthaginian Conquest

Various civilizations, including the Greeks, use the island as a trading post. However, the absence of metal ores deters further colonization until the Carthaginian Empire spreads to this part of the Mediterranean from North Africa in the 7th century BC.

3 Roman Conquest

During the 3rd century BC, Carthage comes into conflict with the expanding Roman Empire. Rome is victorious in 146 BC and establishes order for the next 500 years. In AD 404, Mallorca and its neighbouring islands are established as the province of Balearica.

4 Vandal Invasion

No sooner is the new province officially recognized, however, than Germanic Vandals sweep across the Balearics in about AD 425, swiftly ending Roman rule. So destructive is their takeover that few traces of the Romans' existence are left.

5 Byzantine Conquest

In 533, the Byzantines defeat the Vandals, restoring prosperity and an orthodox form of Christianity. From faraway Constantinople, Emperor Justinian rules the islands as part of the province of Sardinia. They keep this Byzantine connection until the end of the 7th century, then become more or less independent, with close ties to Catalonia.

6 Moorish Conquest

In 902, the Moors occupy the islands and turn them into a fiefdom of the Emirate of Córdoba. Through a succession of dynastic changes, they hold on for 327 years and forcibly convert many inhabitants to Islam.

The arrival of King Jaume I of Aragón

7 The Reconquista

In 1229, King Jaume I of Aragón rises to oppose the Balearic Moors. His forces first land on the western coast of the island at Santa Ponça, from where he marches eastwards to lay siege to Medina Mayurqa (the Moorish name for Palma). The city falls to him on 31 December, after three months.

8 The Kingdom of Mallorca

Despite Jaume's liberal treatment of islanders, and his laws embodied in the Carta de Població, the territory descends into turmoil after his death, due to rivalry between his sons. Eventually, his son Jaume II is restored and succeeded by his son Sancho and Sancho's nephew, Jaume III.

9 Unification with Spain

In 1344, the islands are once again thrown into chaos when united with the Kingdom of Aragón by Pedro IV. Jaume III is killed during a feeble attempt to retake his kingdom. In 1479, following the marriage of Fernando V of Aragón and Isabel I of Castile, Aragón is in turn absorbed into a new Spanish superstate. The islands become a remote outpost, ushering in centuries of decline.

10 Since 1945

Fascist dictator Generalissimo Francisco Franco instigates the development of mass tourism, which brings a much-needed influx of foreign money. This transforms Mallorca from a backwater to one of the 21st century's choicest travel destinations. Tourism becomes the primary industry on the island.

Generalissimo Francisco Franco

TOP 10 HISTORICAL FIGURES

Pedro, son of Jaume I

1 Hannibal
The Carthaginian leader is said to have been born on the island of Cabrera, just off Mallorca (Ibiza and Malta also claim his birthplace).

2 Quintus Metellus
The Roman Consul occupied Mallorca and Menorca in the 2nd century AD.

3 Count Belisarius
The Byzantine general who defeated the Vandals here in AD 533.

4 Emir Abd Allah
This Muslim leader conquered Mallorca and Menorca in the 10th century.

5 Jaume I
The Christian king who took the islands back from the Moors in the 13th century and established remarkably liberal laws in the Carta de Població.

6 Pedro, Son of Jaume I
Jaume I's violent son Pedro and grandson Alfonso III tried to take Mallorca from rightful heir, Jaume II.

7 Jaume II
The rightful heir to Jaume I. He and his descendants carried on Jaume I's legacy until Mallorca was subsumed within the Kingdom of Aragón.

8 Ramon Llull
This great 13th-century mystic, poet and scholar had a profound influence on Mallorcan spiritual life.

9 Robert Graves
The 20th-century English writer *(see p102)*, scholar and poet put Mallorca on the international literary map.

10 Adán Diehl
The Argentinian poet and visionary built the Grand Hotel Formentor *(see p32)* in 1929, marking out Mallorca as an upper-crust tourist destination.

🔟 Ancient Places

Ruins of the necropolis at Son Real

The many watercourses are a distinctly Moorish touch, as well as the little oasis-like groves of trees (see pp28–9) encircling pools, where you can sit and enjoy the fresh air and the music of gurgling rivulets.

1 Necropolis at Son Real

Set on a glorious headland (see p109) on the northern coast, this Talayotic necropolis dates back to the 7th century BC. Most of the funerary objects discovered here were taken to Madrid, but some still remain in a small museum here.

2 Jardins de Alfàbia

Although later Renaissance and Baroque touches are evident in the gardens and house, the underlying Moorish styling predominates.

3 Palau de l'Almudaina, Palma

Many Moorish elements can still be appreciated in the old, rambling palace (see pp12–15) in the capital.

4 Ses Païsses

These Bronze Age remains form one of Mallorca's most impressive prehistoric sites (see p119). The defensive wall, composed of square blocks, is an example of the Mediterranean Cyclopean style – so named by later cultures who believed that only a giant like the Cyclops could have built such a structure.

5 Pollentia

The Moorish town of Alcúdia is built over an ancient Roman settlement called Pollentia (see p35). Little more than a few original Roman columns and foundations remain in situ – after being burned by Vandals in AD 440, the antique structures were dismantled to help create the new town.

The remnants of the ancient Roman settlement of Pollentia

6 Castell del Rei

The Moors chose another picturesque spot for their "Castle of the King". The ruins we see today are the remains of medieval embellishments made by Jaume I. The castle did not effectively defend against pirates, but it was the very last stronghold to surrender to Aragonese invasions in the 14th century *(see p48)*. The interior is not open to the public.

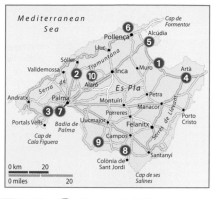

Part of the Banys Àrabs, Palma

7 Banys Àrabs, Palma

These private baths *(see p93)* probably belonged to a wealthy Moorish resident and, together with their gardens, have incredibly survived to this day virtually intact. However, closer examination reveals elements from even earlier sources. The columns, each one different, were doubtless taken from an ancient Roman building.

8 Ses Covetes

Midway along the beach at Es Trénc is the site *(see p122)* of what were probably ancient Roman burial grounds, where cinerary urns containing the ashes of the dead were placed in small niches. Known as a columbarium (from *columba*, Latin for dove), it resembles a pigeon house, with small openings lined up in rows.

9 Capocorb Vell

These well-preserved megalithic ruins *(see p120)*, of the Talayotic culture that dominated the island some 3,000 years ago, are similar to the ones found at Ses Païsses. The word "talayot" refers to the towers at such sites, which were usually two or three storeys high. The central round towers are the oldest elements here; an encircling wall and square towers complete the complex.

10 Castell d'Alaró

This lofty castle *(see p103)* was originally used by the Moors as a stronghold. It proved to be virtually impregnable – conquered only after long sieges, with its defenders eventually being starved out. The Christians refurbished the structure and continued to use it for centuries.

Steps up to Castell d'Alaró

🔟 Monasteries

Carthusian Monastery, Valldemossa

1 Carthusian Monastery, Valldemossa

Set in one of the most appealing towns *(see pp22–3)* on the island, this former monastery and royal residence has a rich history. Most captivating of all to its myriad visitors is the poignant story of the winter visit of Polish composer Frédéric Chopin, sick with tuberculosis, and his lover George Sand, along with her two children – all of whom left copious records of their experiences.

2 Santuari de Sant Salvador

Pilgrims and other visitors can stay overnight at this former monastery *(see p121)*, which has a truly

Santuari de Sant Salvador

spectacular setting, right at the top of the Serres de Llevant mountains. It is difficult to miss: the site's huge stone cross and statue of Christ can be seen for miles around.

3 Santuari de Nostra Senyora de Cura
MAP E4

Ramon Llull *(see p41)* founded this hermitage at the top of the Puig de Randa table mountain in the 13th century, and it was here that he trained missionaries bound for Africa and Asia. Nothing remains of the original building, but Llull's legacy has ensured that the site is an important place for many Catholics. The monastery houses a library and study centre, and visitors are welcome to stay overnight in simple rooms. There are other hermitages lower down the hill.

4 Santuari de Nostra Senyora de Gràcia
MAP E4

The lowest hermitage site on Puig de Randa is set on a ledge in a cliff above a sheer 200-m (656-ft) drop and has beguiling views out over the plain. It was founded in 1497 and appears, along with nesting birds, to be sheltered by the huge rock that overhangs it.

5 Ermita de Sant Llorenç
MAP D2

At Cala Tuent on the island's wild northern coast *(see p112)* is a small

13th-century hermitage perched high above the sea. It was remote at its foundation and remains relatively so today.

6 Ermita de Nostra Senyora de Bonany
MAP F4

This monastery is perched on top of Puig de Bonany. A stone cross was erected here in 1749 for Junípero Serra *(see p127)*, before he left on a mission to California. The sanctuary was built in the 17th century as an act of thanksgiving for a good harvest – *bon any* or "good year". The modern church dates from 1925 and is entered via an imposing gate decorated with ceramic portraits of St Paul and St Anthony. The forecourt has panoramic views.

7 Ermita de Nostra Senyora de Lluc

Not so much an active monastery as a place of pilgrimage that also draws tourists. This is Mallorca's holiest spot *(see p111)*, high in the mountains, and has been a sacred zone since time immemorial. The complex has an attractive church, with a special chapel to house the venerated image of the Virgin Mary. There are also plenty of pilgrim paths to climb and nature trails to explore.

8 Ermita de Nostra Senyora del Puig

Just to the south of Pollença, this serene place *(see p108)* with marvellous views houses one of the oldest Gothic images of the Virgin on the island. The unassuming complex, dating mostly from the 1700s, comprises a courtyard, a chapel, fortified walls, a refectory and cells. Rooms are available to rent.

Wall painting, Ermita de Betlem

9 Ermita de Betlem
MAP G3

Up in the hills northwest of Artà *(see p122)*, this monastery has a lovely vantage point, 400 m (1,312 ft) above the sea. It dates from 1804, when a group of hermits decided to rebuild the church that had been destroyed years before by pirates. The church is tiny and crudely frescoed, but it is worth the detour. The surrounding area has good spots for a picnic.

10 Ermita de Sant Miquel
MAP E4

Just east of Montuïri *(see p128)* is a small monastery with views over the fertile fields of Es Pla. Facilities include a café-restaurant and nicely restored monks' cells, where, for a nominal amount, visitors can stay, as long as they do not mind sharing a bathroom with other guests.

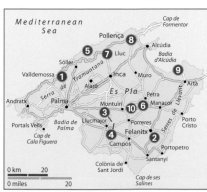

🔟 Churches

1 Sant Bernat, Petra

Petra (see p127) was the birthplace of Fray Junípero Serra, who established Catholic missions all over California in the 1700s and early 1800s. The town's stocky church, Sant Bernat, commemorates the man.

2 Nostra Senyora dels Àngels, Pollença

Features include a rose window with elaborate stone tracery outside, and an intriguing sculpture, located in a side chapel, of St Sebastian nonchalantly resting on the arrows that pierce his body. Note the floor tiles decorated with cockerel heads, the symbol of the town of Pollença (see p110).

3 Església de Santa Eulàlia, Palma

Built just after the Christians reclaimed the Balearics in the 13th century, this church (see p96) has a rare Gothic homogeneity, despite some later medieval touches and a few 19th-century additions.

4 Oratori de Montesió, Porreres

MAP E4

Part of a former monastery, this 14th-century hilltop church overlooks the small agricultural village of Porreres. It has a five-sided cloister, an unusual arcaded façade with elegant Gothic lines, and great views out to sea. The setting makes a wonderful venue for special concerts sponsored by the town, featuring internationally known talents.

5 Nostra Senyora de la Esperança, Capdepera

The story goes that once, when a band of loutish brigands were preparing to attack Capdepera (see p119), the townspeople implored the Madonna to help them. A thick fog promptly settled in, confounding the pirates. Since then, the town's statue has been known as Sa Esperança ("the bringer of hope"). It is housed in a Gothic chapel within the famous castle at Capdepera.

Nostra Senyora dels Àngels, Pollença

6 La Seu, Palma

This grand cathedral *(see pp12–13)* is one of the greatest Gothic churches anywhere. The imposing exterior with flamboyant spires leads into a vast space that houses treasures such as one of the world's largest stained-glass windows.

7 Santuari Ermita de la Victòria

The fortress church *(see p112)* was built on a rocky headland near Alcúdia in the 1600s to house an early statue of the Virgin. Despite these measures, this figure was stolen twice by pirates. The church makes a great starting point for hikes over the promontory.

8 Basílica de Sant Francesc, Palma

Built in 1281 on a site where the Moors made soap, this church *(see p94)* has suffered its share of woes, most notably when struck by lightning in 1580. Consequently, the façade you see today is a Baroque creation, though presumably no less massive than the original Gothic structure. The beautiful cloisters are the star turn, and, in fact, you must go through them first to enter the church.

Altar, Portals Vells Cave Church

9 Portals Vells Cave Church

MAP B5

One of the caves along the rocky headland of Portals Vells has been turned into a church, Cova de la Mare de Déu. According to legend, shipwrecked Genoese sailors who were grateful for their survival began worshipping here. The holy water stoup and altar have been carved out of solid rock, although the effigy of the Virgin that was once here is now in a seafront church at Portals Nous.

10 Nostra Senyora dels Àngels, Sineu

Mallorca's grandest parish church, at the highest point of a town *(see p128)* that was declared the official centre of the island by King Sanç, can be visited only on market day (Wednesday). It has a small archaeological museum.

Nostra Senyora dels Àngels

🔟 Castles and Towers

① Castell de Bellver

One of just a handful of round castles (see pp16–17) in the world, and impeccably preserved, this building conjures up fairy-tale images of damsels in distress and bold knights galloping to the rescue. In fact, its history is a little more prosaic – it was used as a prison for enemies of the Crown for hundreds of years.

② Sant Joan Baptista Belfry

Located in the town of Muro (see p128), this beautiful bell tower seems almost Moorish, so slender is the arch that joins it to the imposing church. However, it sports other elements that recall Gothic and Renaissance styles, including stone carvings, a decorative door and coffers. It is situated in one of the island's prettiest squares.

③ Castell d'Alaró

This remote castle (see p103), found high in the hills on the island's northwest side, was attacked several times over the centuries, each time proving its defences against everything but prolonged siege. Alfonso III, on his invasion of the island, finally took it in 1285. The leaders of the patriots were burned alive by the king, who, in turn, was excommunicated by the pope.

④ Castell del Rei

With Moorish origins and Christian additions, this castle (see p112) never served its defensive purpose well, as raiders simply avoided it. It was demoted to a watchtower, and, in the early 18th century, abandoned altogether. Today, it is a panoramic destination for hikers.

Watchtower on Illa Dragonera

⑤ Tower on Illa Dragonera

The ancient watchtower on one of Mallorca's most picturesque island nature reserves (see p104) may date as far back as Roman times. It may not be much to look at these days, but it's fun just to hike around the unspoiled island and imagine what it must have been like during a raid, with corsairs storming the place and signal fires warning the rest of the island.

⑥ Talaia d'Albercutx

At the highest point on the Península de Formentor is a tower (see p33) that is wondrous for

---

Mediterranean Sea

Cap de Formentor

Pollença ❹ ❻
Lluc
Alcúdia
Sóller
Badia d'Alcúdia
Valldemossa
Inca ❷ Muro
Capdepera
❽
Serra de Tramuntana
❸
Alaró
Es Pla
Artà ❿
Palma ❶
Petra
❺
Andratx
Montuïri
Manacor
Porto Cristo
Portals Vells
Badia de Palma
Porreres
Serres de Llevant
Llucmajor
Felanitx ❾
Cap de Cala Figuera
Campos
Santanyi Portopetro
Colònia de Sant Jordi
❼ ↓ 12 km (7 miles)

0 km   20
0 miles   20

having been built at all in such a precipitous place. At this height, the wind howls, and the views down below are like those from a helicopter. The road to it is perilous, too.

7 Castell de Cabrera
MAP H6 ■ Open daily

The 14th-century castle on the island of Cabrera (see p120), off Mallorca's south coast, has a chequered history, subsequent to its original purpose as a defence measure for the southern reaches of the main island. At various times it has been a pirates' den; a crowded, deadly prison for 9,000 French soldiers in the 19th century; and an outpost for General Franco's Fascist forces in the 20th century. Now the island it oversees is a national park, and stupendous views reward those who climb up to the crumbling old fortress.

8 Torre Verger
Found at the Mirador de Ses Ànimes (see p104), this watchtower, built in 1579, provides what must be among the finest views of the entire western coastline. Visitors can climb up into the stone structure and stand on the topmost level, just as watchmen must have done in the 16th and 17th centuries when Mallorca was subject to almost incessant attack by North African brigands.

The view along the northwest coastline from Torre Verger

Clifftop walls of Castell de Santueri

9 Castell de Santueri
MAP F5 ■ Cami des Castell, Felanitx ■ Open Apr–Sep: 10:30am– 6pm daily ■ Adm

One of several castles with the same name, this one is about 6 km (4 miles) southeast of Felanitx. It was built in the 14th century on the site of a ruined Arab fortress. The view here stretches from the Cap de Formentor to Cabrera. The castle is open to the public following restoration work.

10 Castell de Capdepera
This is another Mallorcan fortress that epitomizes the fairy-tale castle. The approach is a pleasure in itself, as you pass fragrant plants and rocky outcrops, and the views (see p119) are memorable. It was built by King Sanç in the 14th century.

🔟 Modernista Buildings in Palma

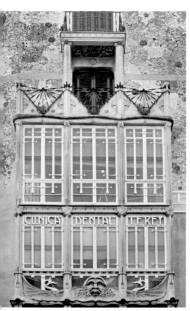

Trencadís mosaic on Can Forteza Rey

① Can Forteza Rey
MAP N3 ■ Plaça del Marquès del Palmer, 1

Local architect Lluís Forteza Rey designed this splendid five-storey apartment building, which is richly decorated in sculptures and *trencadís* (a mosaic of broken tiles). Antoni Gaudí, then working at the cathedral alongside Forteza's father, is said to have contributed ideas for its design.

② Edificio Paraires
MAP L3 ■ Corner of C/Paraires and C/Minyones

The work of local architect Francesc Roca i Simó, this three-storey building features his characteristically refined and restrained style. The most notable features are the large curved windows on each floor, which are decorated with elegant wrought ironwork.

③ Can Roca
MAP M3 ■ C/Sant Nicolau, 18

One of the first Modernista buildings in Palma to use ceramic decoration on its façade, this edifice dates from the turn of the 20th century and is also the work of Francesc Roca i Simó.

④ Parlament (Antiguo Círculo Mallorquín)
MAP L4 ■ C/Conqueridor, 11 ■ 971 228281 ■ Closed Jul (Tue only) & Aug

The Mallorcan parliament occupies a former casino, a 19th-century cultural centre, expanded in 1913 when it was given its elegant Modernista façade. Visits are available (9am–1pm Mon–Fri) but must be booked in advance.

⑤ Forn des Teatre
Modernista architects didn't just design mansions and hotels. The shops also adopted the style. Although the original bakery closed, the new owner is one of the few to retain the Modernista façade, with swirling woodwork, painted panels crowned by a dragon and the iconic sign. The new bakery is called Fornet de la Soca.

Old sign at the entrance to the bakery

6 Gran Hotel

MAP N3 ■ Plaça de Weyler, 3 ■ 971 178512 ■ Open 10am–8pm Mon–Sat, 11am–2pm Sun & hols ■ www.caixaforum.es/palma

The famous Modernista mansion (see p87) was designed by famed architect Lluís Domènech i Montaner, and now houses the CaixaForum. It boasts undulating balconies, tile decoration and an exuberant use of floral motifs. Monthly tours are available but must be pre-booked.

7 Almacenes El Águila

MAP N4 ■ Plaça del Marquès del Palmer, 1

Built in 1908 by Gaspar Bennàssar, this former department store made use of novel construction techniques and materials. Iron columns allowed for the incorporation of vast windows that allowed natural light to flood in. The building also has a lavish façade.

8 Can Casayas and Pension Menorquina

MAP M3 ■ Plaça Mercat

Gaudí's influence is apparent in this charming pair of buildings (designed by Francisco Roca Simó), which exhibit

Can Casayas and Pension Menorquina

his trademark parabolic arches and swooping curves. Plans to connect the two buildings – separated only by a narrow street – with a passage were not approved by the city council.

9 Casa de las Medias

MAP N4 ■ C/Colom, 11

This curious building is covered with the colourful broken tile decoration popularised by the Modernistas. Its name, which means "the house of stockings", comes from the haberdashery that once occupied the ground floor. The five-storey building has unusual pyramid-shaped balconies.

10 Can Corbella

MAP N4 ■ Plaça Cort, 1

The striking horseshoe arches at the entrance here illustrate the Neo-Mudéjar style popular in the late 19th century, and is seen as a precursor to the Modernista movement.

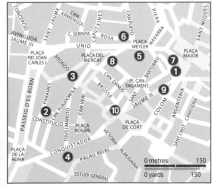

🔟 Museums

Museu Fundación Juan March

1 Museu Fundación Juan March, Palma

A 17th-century mansion *(see p96)*, once the headquarters of the family-owned Banca March, was one of the finer legacies left by founder and Mallorcan financier Juan March. It now houses an extensive exhibition of contemporary Spanish art, including works by Picasso, Miró, Dalí, and Mallorca's greatest living painter, Miquel Barceló.

2 Museu de Lluc

This museum *(see p31)* contains an interesting hotchpotch of prehistoric artifacts, Roman finds, ceramics, religious pieces, and an exhaustive array of works by 20th-century Valldemossan artist Josep Coll Bardolet, who was known for his boldly coloured landscapes.

3 Museu Municipal de Valldemossa

The range of objects on display here *(see pp22–5)* is vast and eclectic, such as the history of printing in Mallorca, the work of an Austrian archduke,

paintings inspired by the mountains of the Tramuntana, and important works by modern masters.

4 Es Baluard

MAP S1 ■ Plaça Porta de Santa Catalina 10 ■ 971 908200 ■ www.esbaluard.org ■ Open 10am–8pm Tue–Sat (until 3pm Sun) ■ Adm

A 16th-century fortress on the waterfront now houses Palma's excellent contemporary art museum. The permanent collection has works by Dalí, Miro and Tàpies among others, and the temporary exhibitions are always interesting. The café enjoys great views over the old city.

5 Fundació Miró Mallorca, Palma

Miró had connections to Mallorca; both his mother and his wife were Mallorcan-born, and the great artist spent the last years of his life here. His studio during that final period has been turned into a museum *(see pp18–19)* devoted to his work.

Exterior of Fundació Miró Mallorca

6 Museu Municipal de Pollença

MAP E1 ■ C/Guillen Cifre de Colonya ■ 971 531166 ■ Open Jun–Sep: 10am–1pm & 5:30–8pm Tue–Sat; Oct–May: 11am–1pm Tue–Sat ■ Adm ■ www.ajpollenca.net/ca/municipi/museu

Exhibits include prehistoric sculptures shaped like bulls and a Tibetan sand painting presented by the Dalai Lama.

artifacts, ceramics, coins, books and paintings spanning the 13th to 16th centuries. Highlights include the jasper sarcophagus of Jaume II, an Arab tombstone and a painting of St George and the Dragon, which presents a background impression of what Palma may have looked like during the 15th-century.

7 Museu de Mallorca, Palma

The palace that houses this excellent museum (see p93) dates from 1634. The collections present a full and well-documented range of Mallorcan artifacts, from the prehistoric up to fine examples of Modernista furniture. The Talayot figures – small bronze warriors – and re-creations of Neolithic dwellings are among the other highlights.

Votive statuette, Museu de Mallorca

8 Museu Diocesà, Palma

Housed in the former Episcopal Palace, this treasure trove (see p95) contains numerous archaeological

9 Museu Monogràfic, Alcúdia

MAP F2 ■ C/Sant Jaume, 30 ■ 971 547004 ■ Open 9:30am–3pm Mon–Fri ■ Adm

This small but beautifully designed museum houses all the finds from ancient Roman Pollentia, such as cult figures, surgical instruments, jewellery and gladiatorial gear.

10 Fundación Yannick y Ben Jakober, near Alcúdia

MAP F2 ■ C/ de la Victoria; ■ Open 10am–6pm Mon–Sat ■ Adm

Set amid a rose garden and sculpture park, the foundation houses contemporary art and royal child portraits from the 16th to 19th centuries.

A Swarovski crystal curtain donated to the Fundación Yannick y Ben Jakober

🔟 Villages

1 Algaida
MAP D4

Most people will pass through the outskirts of this small town on their way to Puig de Randa, but it is well worth making a stop here for some good restaurants *(see p131)*, where the people of Palma come to dine at weekends. The Gordiola Glassworks *(see p129)* are also nearby.

2 Santanyí
Founded in 1300 by King Jaume II, Santanyí *(see p122)* was given a protective wall due to its proximity to the coast. Only part of that wall remains, but it gives the place a certain character. For this reason, the town has attracted a large number of foreign dwellers, who have turned it into a lively, rather cosmopolitan place. The art galleries on the main square are well worth checking out.

Street market in Santanyí

3 Alaró
MAP D3

At one end of a scenic mountain road, under the shadow of the Castell d'Alaró *(see p103)*, this pleasant little town dates from at least the time of the Moors. If you want to climb up to the castle, drive up to Es Verger restaurant and proceed on foot: the ascent takes about 45 minutes and the view is marvellous.

Quiet street in Fornalutx's old town

4 Fornalutx
Often voted Mallorca's loveliest village *(see p101)* – if not all of Spain's – this enchanting mountain enclave was founded by the Moors in the 12th century. The tiny village square is a friendly gathering place, but it is the heady views that visitors remember the most – up to the island's highest mountain and down into a verdant valley below.

5 Estellencs
Though today it is a pretty terraced town *(see p104)* in a magnificent mountain setting, its old houses of grey-brown stone – left unplastered and unadorned – were essentially built for defence. Even the 15th-century church belfry was used as a place of refuge, as were most towers on the island.

6 Santa Maria del Camí
MAP D3

A way station for weary travellers over the centuries, the village has a charming Baroque belfry, the Convent dels Mínims, a famed Sunday market and a quaintly traditional textile factory *(see p130)*.

7 Orient

Again, it is the mountain setting that dazzles here: this tiny, remote hamlet (see p104), with some 40 houses, a couple of restaurants and a church, has some of the finest views the island has to offer. It is also used as an excellent base for hikers or anyone who just wants to breathe the exhilarating air.

8 Binissalem

This small town (see p127) is probably second only to Palma in the number and splendour of its stately mansions. Most of them date from the 18th century, when the surrounding area became the centre of a booming wine business. All of that stopped at the end of the 19th century, when phylloxera wiped out the vines. The local wine industry was revived in the late 20th century by the growing demand for good-quality local wines.

9 Capdepera

The extremely large and well-preserved medieval fortress that dominates the ridge above the town (see p119) is the main reason to come to Capdepera. With its crenellated walls draped over the rolling hilltop, it is certainly a noble sight and one of Mallorca's finest castles. A fort has existed here in some form since at least the Roman times, and it has more or less been continuously used throughout centuries of international squabbles and raids by pirates.

10 Deià

Spilling down a steep hillside, Deià's (see p102) earth-tone-coloured houses are, to many, the finest on the island. English poet and writer Robert Graves (1895–1985) lived here until his death, and he and his many artistic friends brought international fame to this picturesque village. Today, the tiny artists' retreat has been bought up by the wealthy, though it still retains its traditional appearance.

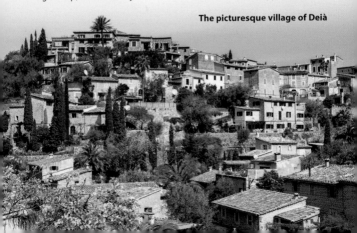

The picturesque village of Deià

TOP 10 **Ports and Resorts**

2 Platja de Canyamel
MAP H3

If a tranquil resort sounds enticing, this might be the place to come. Even in high season, it remains a quiet, family-oriented place – just a curving sandy beach backed by pine woods and a few tasteful hotels.

3 Port de Pollença

This family-friendly resort (see p110), situated 6 km (4 miles) to the northeast of Pollença, beside a pleasant bay, is an attractive place with a long, sandy beach. Many retired foreigners have made the town their home.

1 Port de Valldemossa
MAP C3

This is more a cove than a port. The beach here is pebbly, and the houses are made of stone, as are the villas that are dotted all across the hill. Getting here involves a challenging drive down a series of hairpin bends along a cliff face and through pine forests. The lone restaurant, Es Port, is a treat, though only open for lunch.

4 Cala Fornells
MAP B4

A pleasant resort, Cala Fornells is made up of coves with turquoise water, sandy beaches and large, flat rocks on which to bask. Families flock here, and it's very good for snorkelling. The nearby town of Peguera has good nightlife.

Turquoise waters of Cala Fornells

Alfresco lunch, Port d'Andratx

⑤ Port d'Andratx

One of the classiest resort ports (see p104) on the island, it is frequented by the Spanish king and other eminent visitors. Most of the restaurants and shops are on the south side of the port, while there is a prestigious sailing club on the north. The water is an inviting mix of azure and lapis, with touches of emerald, but the only beach is tiny.

⑥ Porto Cristo

Set around an old fishing harbour on the east coast, this family-friendly resort (see p122) has something for everyone. Choose from Blue Flag beaches, shops and restaurants, or the nearby archae-ological sites and the famous Coves del Drac.

⑦ Cala Ratjada

This place (see p122) is ideal for watersports of all kinds. Until recently the town was a quaint fish-ing village, and though it still has a working fishing port it is now rather overdeveloped. Fine beaches nearby include Cala Guyá, Cala Mezquida and Cala Torta, which allows nudists.

⑧ Port d'Alcúdia

Big and a bit brash, this resort town (see p110) is a hit with the party-goers. There are things most visitors might prefer to do without – fast food joints and too many fluores-cent lights creating a ghostly pallor along the promenade by night. Still, the beaches here are good, some of the restaurants are excellent and the nightlife's non-stop.

⑨ Portopetro
MAP F6

Although on the verge of being swallowed whole by Cala d'Or (see p122), this little fishing village has so far managed to retain its original flavour – possibly because there is no beach. Visitors can walk around and admire the slopes dotted by villas and the boats in the small marina. There is only one hotel in town, which makes a good base from which to explore the island.

Beachgoers at Port de Sóller

⑩ Port de Sóller

The lovely bay here (see p100) offers calm waters for swimming, and a pedestrian walk lines the beaches. The resort hotels and nightlife venues cater to both young and old. Try not to miss a ride on the antique tram that scoots to and from downtown Sóller.

🔟 Areas of Natural Beauty

Brilliant blue waters of the man-made reservoir on Gorg Blau

1 Gorg Blau

Created by seasonal torrents over millions of years, the ravine near Sóller and Puig Major is up to 400 m (1,312 ft) deep but only 30 m (98 ft) wide, with some sections never seeing daylight. A man-made reservoir here supplies water to Palma. Do not hike (see p70) between the cliffs in winter.

2 Península de Formentor

This jagged spur of the great Serra de Tramuntana range has

Spectacular Península de Formentor

been preserved and saved from overdevelopment mostly due to the fact that a large luxury hotel was built here (see pp32–3) in the 1920s. The drive out to the lighthouse from Port de Pollença is absolutely unforgettable.

3 Torrent de Pareis

A box canyon at the spot (see p112) where the "Torrent of the Twins" meets the sea is one of the great sights of the island. The scale of the scene, with its delicate formations and colours, is amazing, and the sense of solitude is totally undisturbed, even by the usual crowds you will encounter here. The tunnel-like path from Cala Calobra was carved out in 1950.

4 Parc Natural de Mondragó

One of the newer nature reserves (see p120) established on the island, this one is part nature, part heritage site. It incorporates a full range of island terrains, from wooded hills to sandy dunes, as well as an assortment of rural structures. Come here for hiking, bird-watching, picnicking, swimming or simply getting a feel for old Mallorca.

5 Mirador de Ricardo Roca

MAP B3

A chapel-like structure at this lookout point has the words *todo por la patria* (all for the father-land) inscribed over its door – a remnant from Fascist times – with *patria* deleted some time ago by a liberal-thinking member of the new Spain. From here, there are dizzying views down to the sea below.

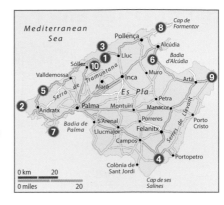

6 Parc Natural de S'Albufera

Roman naturalist Pliny wrote of Mallorcan night herons, probably from S'Albufera, being sent to Rome as a gastronomic delicacy. Most of the wetlands were drained for agri-culture in the 19th century and what land was left has now been restored and turned into the largest wetlands nature reserve in the Balearics.

7 Cap de Cala Figuera Peninsula

MAP B5

Marked by a lonely lighthouse, this undeveloped area is officially a military zone, but as long as it is not closed or guarded it is possible to walk out for a view of the bay. Nearby Portals Vells is a tranquil area, while Platja El Mago is a nudist beach.

8 Illa Dragonera

This uninhabited island *(see p104)* is the place that encouraged the current conservation movement on the island. It is a great place to hike, take a picnic or just visit to admire the natural beauty. In the high season, ferries head here from either Sant Elm or Port d'Andratx.

9 Cap de Capdepera

MAP H3

The island's easternmost point is a great place to hike around, though the terrain generally necessitates little more than easy strolling.

Visitors can go out to the lighthouse on its cape of sheer rock, or check out the pristine coves that lie lined up to the north and south, including Cala Agulla, Son Moll, Sa Pedruscada and Sa Font de sa Cala.

10 Barranc de Biniaraix

MAP C2

This is one of the island's most popular and breathtaking walks. Follow the cobbled pathways from the tiny village of Biniaraix up through the impressive scenery overlooked by Puig Major, Mallorca's highest mountain.

Mountains behind Biniaraix

🔟 Beaches and Coves

Crowds filling the beach at Cala Sant Vicenç in June

1 Cala Sant Vicenç

The area consists of three coves – Cala Sant Vicenç (see p110), Cala Barques and Cala Molins – with an appealing sense of intimacy. The first two have tiny but perfect beaches, gorgeous water and views. The third is down a hill, with a broader beach and more privacy.

2 Palmanova
MAP B4

Lying in the southwest of the island, Palmanova is only a few miles from Palma, with all its attractions. It makes an excellent staging post for family activities, such as visits to nearby Aqualand Water Park or Marineland (see pp72–3). The town's superb sandy beach is renowned.

3 Cova Blava (Blue Grotto)
MAP H6

This pretty little waterside cave is incorporated as part of the return trip to the Illa de Cabrera (see p120). Like its famous forerunner on the isle of Capri in Italy, this Blue Grotto offers the amazing spectacle of the outside light being filtered up through the aquamarine waters, creating a luminosity that seems at once spectral, gem-like and spectacular. Visitors can swim here, too.

4 Illetes
MAP C4

The western side of Palma Bay is generally upmarket, and "The Islets" typify the area's allure. Tiny islands, intimate coves, rocky cliffs and rolling hillsides are accentuated with attractive villas and a scattering of exclusive hotels on the waterfront.

Mediterranean Sea

Cap de Formentor
Pollença
Alcúdia
Lluc
Badia d'Alcúdia
Cala Rajada
Sóller
Valldemossa
Muro
Artà
Inca
Es Pla
Andratx
Alaró
Palma
Petra
Montuïri
Manacor
Porto Cristo
Portals Vells
Porreres
Felanitx
Llucmajor
Badia de Palma
Cap de Cala Figuera
Campos
Santanyí
Portopetro
Colònia de Sant Jordi

0 km 20
0 miles 20

3 ↓ 12 km (7 miles)

5 Cala Tuent
On the wild northwest coast, where the opalescent hues of the massive cliffs and sea meet, Cala Tuent *(see p112)* is probably the area's quietest beach, since it is bypassed by most of the crowds of tourists who come to see the nearby Torrent de Pareis *(see p112)*.

6 Es Trenc
MAP E6
This splendid beach is everyone's favourite, and weekends will find it very crowded with sun-worshippers who have made the trip from Palma. The rest of the week, it is the domain of nudists, nature-lovers, and neo-hippies. It remains the island's last undeveloped beach, interrupted only by the complex of vacation homes at Ses Covetes *(see p122)*.

7 Platja de Formentor
Day-trippers from Port de Pollença love to come here, either by car or ferry, to partake of the same pristine sands and pure waters as the guests of the grand Hotel Barceló Formentor *(see p32)*. The unspoiled views here are among the very best on the island.

8 Cala Deià
MAP C2
Hidden away among the mountains of the northwest coast, Cala Deià occupies a narrow rocky cove with a shingle beach. It is a favourite spot with local expats, who linger at the very informal beachside café.

9 Cala Figuera, Cap de Formentor
MAP F1
Cutting a chunk out of the very end of the dramatic Península de Formentor, this cove *(see p32)* lies at the bottom of a precipitous ravine. It is accessible either on foot – parking is up above, just off the road that winds out to the lighthouse – or by boat, anchored offshore. Once there, the views of the surrounding cliffs are awesome, and the beach and water make it one of the island's most inviting swimming spots.

Cala Figuera, Cap de Formentor

10 Cala Millor
MAP G4
One of the most popular resorts on the east coast of Mallorca. The first hotels began to appear here as early as the 1930s, but the real tourist invasion did not start until the 1980s. Similar to neighbouring Cala Bona and Sa Coma, Cala Millor has several beautiful beaches; the main one is 1.8 km (1 mile) long and is quite magnificent. There are bars, restaurants and clubs aplenty, all of which become overcrowded in summer. To see what this coast used to be like, walk to the headland at Punta de N'Amer nature reserve.

Clear blue waters at Cala Deià

🔟 Parks and Gardens

Cactus assortment at Botanicactus

(see p102) was his favourite. The gardens, terraced in the ancient Moorish fashion, are deliberately left a bit wild, in keeping with the slightly rough look of the natural flora. All this vibrant nature neatly contrasts with the refinement of the architecture, especially the gazebo that offers exquisitely perfect views of the coast.

① Botanicactus
MAP E6 ■ Ctra de Ses Salines a Santanyí, Ses Salines ■ 971 649494 ■ Open Mar: 9am–6:30pm daily; Apr–Aug: 9am–7:30pm daily; Sep & Oct: 9am–7pm daily; Nov–Feb: 10:30am–4:30pm daily ■ Adm

One of Europe's largest botanical gardens, Botanicactus has 12,000 cacti to admire, including a 300-year-old giant from Arizona. There are also palms, bamboo groves and a large lake. Local flora is showcased through olive trees, pomegranates, almonds, pines, oranges, carobs and cypresses.

② Son Marroig
The famous Archduke Luis Salvador *(see p24)* had many homes in Mallorca, but Son Marroig

③ Banys Àrabs Gardens
To the Moors, who came from an arid land where the oasis was the symbol of life, water was the very essence of a garden. The cloistered gardens surrounding the Banys Àrabs *(see p93)* evoke that ideal – it was here that the wealthy owner would relax after his bath, and breathe in the fragrant air.

④ Jardins Sa Torre Cega
C/Juan March 2, Capdepera ■ MAP H3 ■ Visits arranged by the Tourist Office ■ 971 819467 ■ Adm

Joan March was a native-born magnate who allegedly made his fortune from illegal tobacco and arms trafficking. His old mansion, built in 1916, near Cala Ratjada, has lavish grounds incorporating water gardens, pine woods and fruit groves. The gardens are also home to an impressive collection of over 40 works of modern sculpture, including a bronze by Rodin and a piece by Henry Moore.

View from the gazebo at Son Marroig

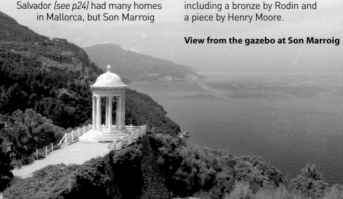

5 Jardins de Alfàbia

The island's best example of a profoundly Moorish garden *(see p28)* dates back 1,000 years. Naturally, in all those centuries the various owners have added their own touches, resulting in Renaissance and Baroque elements in the design.

6 Parc de la Mar

With its artificial lake, section of city walls and great views, this *(see p96)* is a lovely place to stroll at any time. At night, the sparkling city lights of Palma and warm glow of the nearby cathedral and palaces add a magical quality.

Palm trees at the Jardí Botànic

7 Jardí Botànic

MAP C2 ■ Ctra Palma-Sóller, km 30.5, Sóller ■ 971 634014 ■ Open Mar–Oct: 10am–6pm Tue–Sat; Nov–Feb: 10am–2pm Tue–Sat ■ Closed Dec ■ Adm

Founded in 1985 for the conservation and study of Mediterranean flora, the garden is home to many endangered plants. Find medicinal herbs and flowers, wild flora and vegetables here.

8 Raixa

These gardens belonged to a cardinal, who liberally indulged his taste for collecting Classical statuary *(see p102)*. However, only a fraction of his collection remains in the gardens; the rest now adorns the Castell de Bellver *(see pp16–17)* in Palma.

9 Parque de la Feixina

MAP J3

These gardens start where Avinguda Argentina meets the Avinguda de Gabriel Roca, and run up to Plaça La Feixina. The terraced lawns, fragrant trees and flowers, and attractive fountains and columns provide a welcome respite from the stone and asphalt of the newer parts of Palma.

10 S'Hort del Rei

MAP L5

Gentle jets of water and bowl-shaped fonts characterize this lovely Moorish-influenced garden. As the name suggests, it was once the king's private garden. Today, it is home to some eccentric modern sculpture.

Water feature at S'Hort del Rei

📟 Wildlife and Plants

Dwarf fan palms overlooking the Cap de Capdepera

1 Trees
The mountain areas are defined by pines, junipers, carobs and evergreen holm oaks, while palms, yews and cypress have been planted on the island since time immemorial.

2 Herbs and Shrubs
These include the wild grass (*Ampelodesma mauritanica*), used for thatching and rope; the Balearics' only native palm, the dwarf fan palm; giant yucca and aloe; palmetto, used for basketry; and the giant fennel plant.

3 Mammals
Plenty of wild mountain goats can be seen in the remote areas of Mallorca. Rabbits, hares, hedgehogs, civet cats, ferrets, weasels and other small creatures may take longer to spot. The Mallorcan donkey is also increasingly rare – it has been

Mallorcan donkey under an olive tree

crossbred with its Algerian cousin, and there are only a handful of members of the pure species in existence.

4 Insects
In the warmer seasons, there are plenty of colourful butterflies in the wooded areas of the island, as well as bees, mayflies and hornets. In hot weather, especially among cedars, hikers will be treated to the noisy song of the cicadas.

5 Marine Birds
Bird-watchers come from all over Europe to see rare migrants, especially at the S'Albufera wetlands (see p110). Notable species include marsh harriers, herons, egrets, stilts, bitterns and flamingos. Seagulls, sandpipers, cormorants, ospreys and terns live along the rocky coasts.

6 Songbirds
Species breeding here, or stopping for a visit in the spring or summer, include stonechats, larks, warblers, the stripy hoopoe, swifts, partridges, buntings, finches, pipits, shrikes, turtle doves, swallows, the brilliantly coloured European bee-eater and the inimitable nightingale.

7 Wild Flowers
The island is home to more than 1,300 varieties of flowering

plants, of which 40 are uniquely Mallorcan. Look out especially for the asphodel (with its tall spikes and clusters of pink flowers), the rock rose in the Serra de Tramuntana and the Balearic peonies. Spring and early summer are usually the best times to see them in all their colourful bounty.

8 Reptiles and Amphibians

Frogs, salamanders, tortoises, snakes and lizards abound. But perhaps the most notable two species on the island are the endangered ferreret, a toad found in the Serra de Tramuntana, and Lilford's wall lizard, which thrives on the islets offshore.

9 Cultivated Plants

Some of the flowering plants you see around the island are cultivated for decorative purposes, such as oleander, purple morning glory, bougainvillea, *Bignonia jasminoides* (trumpet vine – used as cover for pergolas), geranium and wisteria. Grapes, citrus fruit, almonds and olives have been part of Mallorca's landscape since Roman times.

10 Birds of Prey

The island's numerous dashing Eleanora's falcons form an important part of the world's population – you can see them around the Formentor lighthouse (see p32). The peregrine falcon, too, breeds in these parts, and you can spot black vultures, red kites, eagles, buzzards, harriers and owls.

Red kite, Serra de Tramuntana

TOP 10 PLACES TO SEE WILDLIFE

Península de Formentor lighthouse

1 Península de Formentor
This jagged spur of mountain and rock (see pp32–3) is circled by seabirds, including the stunning Eleanora's falcon.

2 Illa de Cabrera
This sun-bleached archipelago (see p120) off the island's south coast is famous for its colony of Lilford's wall lizards.

3 Gorg Blau
This remote gorge (see p108), surrounded by mighty peaks, is the best place to spot the rare black vulture.

4 S'Albufera
A rare patch of wetland, S'Albufera (see p110) is a haven for many types of bird, including crakes and herons.

5 Sineu
In fields near Sineu (see p128) you could spy the brightly coloured hoopoe, one of Mallorca's handsomest birds.

6 Sa Dragonera
An uninhabited nature reserve off the west coast, Sa Dragonera (see p104) is famous for its spectacular seabirds, notably ospreys and shags.

7 Lluc
The mountains near Lluc (see pp30–31) are the last refuge for the rare and endangered ferreret.

8 Es Pla
It's rare to catch sight of the nightingale but you may hear this shy bird singing in any part of Es Pla (see pp126–9).

9 Colonia de Sant Jordi
The saltpans behind this resort (see p121) have a distinctive birdlife, including flamingos and black-winged stilts.

10 Parc Natural de Mondragó
This lovely nature reserve and park (see p120) attracts a wide variety of migratory and resident birds.

🔟 Walks and Drives

Drivers navigate the windy Sa Calobra road in the shadow of Puig Major

1 La Reserva (Walk)
MAP B3 ■ 2 hours ■ Adm

This reserve on the slopes of Puig de Galatzó has Mallorca's most diverse collection of plants. A 3.5-km (2-mile) trail takes in waterfalls and springs.

2 Sant Elm to La Trapa (Walk)
MAP A4 ■ 3 hours for whole route

This popular walk leads to an old Trappist monastery. A shorter route is signposted beside the cemetery on the Sant Elm–Andratx road.

3 GR-221 Long-Distance Route (Walk)
A beautiful walk that follows the length of the Sierra de Tramuntana on the island's northwest coast (see p135). Around 135 km (84 miles) long, it takes about 6 to 8 days to complete.

Signpost on the GR-221 route

4 Sa Calobra (Drive)
MAP D2 ■ About 30 minutes

Driving anywhere around Puig Major (see p112) affords great views and challenges your driving skills. With looping turns that twist down the mountainside, this road has earned its name, which translates as "The Snake". It leads to a tiny settlement, where you can explore the dazzling beauties of the box canyon created over thousands of years by surging torrents.

5 Andratx Round Trip (Drive)
MAP B3–4 ■ 2 hours

Take the main highway north of Andratx to the Mirador de Ricardo Roca, Banyalbufar, then Mirador de Ses Ànimes (see p104) for stunning panoramic views. Turn towards La Granja, then pass down through Puigpunyent, Puig de Galatzo, Galilea, Es Capdellà and back to Andratx.

6 Old Road to Sóller (Drive)
MAP C3 ■ About 45 minutes

The drive over the Coll de Sóller, with its 57 hairpin bends, is Mallorca's most exhilarating. But it is worth it to experience what life used to be like before the tunnel opened.

Previous pages Marble gazebo at Son Marroig

Walks and Drives « **69**

⑦ Puig de Santa Eugènia (Walk)

MAP D3 ▪ 2 hours to top

From the village of Santa Eugènia, walk to Ses Coves. From here, a series of tracks takes you up to a pass and the cross on the summit of Puig de Santa Eugènia, affording fine views.

⑧ Archduke's Mulepath (Walk)

MAP C3 ▪ Near Valldemossa ▪ 6 hours

Red markers take you up to a viewpoint and a high plateau before dropping down through a wooded valley. For experienced hikers only.

Puig Maria, as seen from Pollença

⑨ Pollença to Puig de Maria (Walk)

MAP E1–2 ▪ 90 minutes to top

The signpost to Puig de Maria is at km 52 on the main road from Palma to Pollença. A sanctuary, set on an isolated hill, offers stirring views of the Península de Formentor.

⑩ Bunyola–Orient–Alaró (Drive)

MAP C3–D3 ▪ About 1 hour with stops

Another extremely narrow road that threads its way along precipitous mountain ridges. The town of Orient is a pretty eagle's nest of a place, and the glimpse of Castell d'Alaró (see p48) will fire your imagination.

TOP 10 PEAKS

1 Puig Major
MAP D2 ▪ 1,447 m (4,747 ft)
The island's highest mountain (see p112) is part of the Tramuntana range.

2 Puig Sant Salvador
MAP F5 ▪ 510 m (1,673 ft)
The second-highest peak in the Serra de Llevant is home to the well-loved Santuari de San Salvador (see p44).

3 Puig de ses Bassetes
MAP D2 ▪ 1,216 m (3,990 ft)
Southwest of Massanella, this peak is near the Gorg Blau reservoir.

4 Puig d'es Teix
MAP C2 ▪ 1,062 m (3,484 ft)
A mountain in the heart of the most verdant part of the Tramuntana.

5 Puig Galatzó
MAP B3 ▪ 1,025 m (3,363 ft)
This overlooks the picturesque valley of Puigpunyent, north of Palma.

6 Puig Roig
MAP D1 ▪ 1,002 m (3,287 ft)
Just north of the holy site of Lluc, this peak is named for its reddish colour.

7 Puig Caragoler
MAP D1 ▪ 906 m (2,972 ft)
Access is via Camí Vell de Lluc, a trail used to reach Lluc Monastery.

8 Puig Morell
MAP G3 ▪ 560 m (1,837 ft)
Good for hiking, this is the highest peak in the Serres de Llevant.

9 Puig de Randa
MAP F5 ▪ 543 m (1,781 ft)
The only high point on the Central Plain, and the site of Santuari de Nostra Senyora de Cura (see p44).

10 Puig de Massanella
MAP D2 ▪ 1,367 m (4,485 ft)
This is the highest mountain that can actually be climbed on the island.

Towering Puig de Massanella

ᴛᴏᴘ10 Outdoor Activities and Sports

Hiking to the Cala S'Almonia

① Hiking

Mallorca's most challenging long-distance footpath is the GR-221, which weaves a dramatic route across the mountains of the Sierra de Tramuntana. It takes up to 8 days to complete the full trail. There are scores of other shorter trails leading through stunning scenery.

② Cycling

Groups of avid cyclists, decked out in their colourful lycra, are seen all over the island, from the twistiest mountain roads to the narrowest stone-walled lanes of Es Pla. It is easy to rent bicycles in most towns.

③ Fútbol

There are two professional football teams in Mallorca – Real Mallorca and Atlético Baleares – both of whom play in Palma during the season, which runs from early September to April.

④ Canyoning

A key target for canyoning enthusiasts is the Torrent de Pareis, a dramatic gorge that cuts through the mountains backing onto Sa Calobra. The area can be dangerous and is suitable only for experienced canyoners with the proper equipment.

⑤ Rock Climbing

There are many compelling challenges for climbers on the rocky cliffs that abound along the length of the Serra de Tramuntana, from Sóller in the west to the end of the Península de Formentor in the east. Parks and tourist offices offer published guidelines for tackling the wilderness.

⑥ Fishing

There are a number of boats that will take people out fishing for the day, particularly from the port towns that still fish commercially, such as Portocolom *(see p122)*. The bays of Pollença and Alcúdia *(see p110)* are also popular for fishing.

Cycling the island's mountain roads

7 Horse-Riding

Mallorcan farmers are proud of their well-bred horses, and horse-riding is a very popular pastime in Mallorca. The best place to get in the saddle is in the Serres de Llevant, a gentle band of hills on the eastern side of the island, where you will find several good-quality riding schools.

8 Paragliding

Seeing the island from the air is a thrilling and unforgettable experience, and there is no better way to do it than from ta paraglider. Mallorca now boasts several tour operators and paragliding schools, with options for all levels.

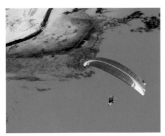

Paragliding over the Mallorcan coast

9 Golf

Golf Son Termens: Bunyola: 971 617862 ▪ Capdepera Golf: 971 818500 ▪ Club de Golf Vall d'Or: Portocolom-Cala d'Or; 971 837001
There are more than 20 world-class golf courses scattered all around the island. Courses are prevalent near all the the big resorts, though some of the finer hotels have their own and many more have putting greens.

10 Bird-Watching

Nature reserves are best for bird sightings, especially those on the northeastern coast, such as S'Albufera (see p110) and the Península de Formentor (see pp32–3). Spring and autumn are optimal times to visit, when migratory birds use Mallorca as a staging post between Europe and Africa. The isolated islands of Sa Dragonera (see p104) and Cabrera (see p120) are also excellent for spotting.

TOP 10 MARINE ACTIVITIES AND WATERSPORTS

Jet skiing in Mallorca

1 Jet Skiing
Among many of the larger resorts, you can rent a jet ski at Magaluf and Port d'Alcúdia (see p110). Rev up the engine and off you go.

2 Scuba Diving
The waters off Mallorca tend to have poor visibility – but the waters off Illa Dragonera (see p104) are crystal clear.

3 Windsurfing
The windy waters in the bay beside Port de Pollença (see p110) are very popular with windsurfers.

4 Boating
Cruises of every sort are popular on Mallorca, but the finest are the 2- or 3-hour cruises along the dramatic southeast coast (see pp118–21).

5 Diving
The clear coastal waters off Estellencs (see p104) provide some of the best diving conditions on the island.

6 Sea-Kayaking
Several companies offer sea-kayaking trips with a favourite spot being the bay edging Port de Sóller (see p100).

7 Water Skiing
All of Mallorca's larger resorts cater for would-be water skiers.

8 Paddle Boarding
Something of a minority interest on the island at present, paddle boarding is becoming increasingly popular.

9 Pedalos
Gone are the days of simple and basic pedalos – now you can rent large and brightly coloured versions in the shape of cars and yachts at most large resorts.

10 Sailing
The myriad coves and bays of Mallorca are perfect for sailors – and sailing.

🔟 Children's Attractions

Large fish tank at Palma Aquarium

1 Palma Aquarium

MAP C4 ■ C/Manuela de los Herreros i Sorà, 21 ■ 902 702902 ■ Open 9:30am–6:30pm daily (last entry 5pm) ■ Adm

This aquarium is home to a range of flora and fauna from the world's largest oceans and the Mediterranean Sea. Ecosystems of 700 species and 8,000 specimens are re-created here.

2 Aqualand

MAP B4

■ Autovía Palma–Arenal, km 15, El Arenal ■ Open May, Jun, Sep & Oct: 10am–5pm daily; Jul & Aug: 10am–6pm daily ■ www.aqualand.es

Mallorca's largest waterpark is a real hit with the kids – both tourists and local. There are swimming pools, water flumes and chutes galore, with one resembling a giant, wriggling snake.

3 Sport Xperience by Rafa Nadal

MAP F4 ■ Cales de Mallorca s/n, Manacor ■ 971 171683 ■ Adm

Sports enthusiasts will enjoy this immersive museum. Interactive and high-tech exhibits bring to life sports from Formula 1 to tennis. Tennis fans should not miss Rafael Nadal's huge collection of trophies and rackets. The centre also has a sports complex, tennis school, hotel and places to eat at.

4 Rancho Grande

MAP F3 ■ Son Serra de Marina, Ctra Arta-Alcúdia, km 13.7, Santa Margalida ■ 971 854121 ■ Adm ■ www.ranchograndemallorca.com

The largest horse ranch on Mallorca offers rides for people of all ages and evening entertainment for the whole family. There are also wagon rides, a children's play area, a mini-zoo, and a bar and restaurant.

5 Karting Magaluf

MAP B4 ■ Ctra de la Porrasa, Magaluf, Calvià ■ 971 131734 ■ Open Nov–15 Dec & 16 Jan–Easter: 10am–6pm Wed–Sun; Easter–mid-Jun & mid-Sep–Oct: 11am–8pm daily; mid-Jun–mid-Sep: 10am–10pm Mon–Sat, noon–9pm Sun ■ Adm ■ www.kartingmagaluf.com

Karting Magaluf

An exhilarating karting experience for the family. Safe and secure tracks and go-karts are suited to children as young as three years old, and everyone is made to feel like a champion. A large terrace bar is available for snacks, drinks and ice creams.

The vast upside-down House of Katmandu, great fun for kids

6 House of Katmandu

MAP B4 ■ Avda. Pedro Vaquer Ramis, 9, Magaluf, Calviá ■ 971 134660 ■ Open from 10am daily ■ Closed Nov–Jan: Mon & Tue ■ Adm ■ www.katmandupark.com

This enormous, fun upside-down Tibetan-style house has been voted the second most popular family attraction in Mallorca. It is full of interactive games and has a 4D cinema, a water-park and a mini-golf course.

7 Golf Fantasía

MAP B4 ■ C/Tenis, 3, Palmanova, Calviá ■ 971 135040 ■ Open Nov–Mar: 10am–6pm daily; Apr, May & Oct: 10am–10pm daily; Jun–Sep: 10am–midnight daily ■ Adm ■ www.golffantasia.com

Just metres from the beach, Golf Fantasía offers family fun with three 18-hole courses set among caves, wooden bridges, waterfalls and tropical gardens with ducks and turtles. There is also a terrace snack bar.

8 Tram from Sóller to Port de Sóller

MAP C2 ■ Tram departs every hour daily (from Soller: 8am–8:30pm; from Port de Soller: 8:30am–9pm) ■ Adm

Board a slow tram at the little station above the main square of Sóller, which takes visitors 5 km (3 miles) through the town and along the water's edge to Port de Sóller. The cars are ex-San Francisco rolling stock from the 1930s.

9 Caves

Young adventurers will love the thrill of exploring Mallorca's caves, especially the Coves d'Artà (see p119), which exit onto the open sea. At the Coves del Drac (see pp36–7), the pitch-darkness is exciting, but the very young may find it a little scary, or get frustrated by the silence.

10 Western Water Park

MAP B4 ■ Ctra Cala Figuera-Sa Porrasa 2–22, Magaluf ■ 971 131203 ■ Open late May–Oct: 10am–5pm daily; Jul & Aug: 10am–6pm daily ■ Adm ■ www.westernpark.com

Mallorca's most popular waterpark has a kitsch western theme with a saloon and a candy parlour. It is also home to the highest waterslide on the island – the so-called "Beast".

Rides at Western Water Park, Magaluf

🔟 **Bars and Nightclubs**

Luxurious interiors of Puro Beach

❶ Puro Beach, Palma Bay

This is a chic, Ibiza-style hang-out by the sea, with a cool lounge bar, music, regular DJs and laid-back poolside dining. Spa treatments are also available by day and night. It's a classy spot *(see p98)*, so you will fit in better if you dress to impress.

❷ Bar Flexas, Palma

Vintage-style distressed furnishings and fittings along with eye-catching paintings on the wall characterize this bar *(see p98)*. It attracts a young and avant-garde clientele, who come to drink until the early hours of the morning.

❸ Galactic Club, Palma

MAP C4 ▪ C/Murillo 9 ▪ 678 017105 ▪ Open 8am–2pm & 8pm–2am Mon–Fri, 8am–2am Sat

Offering a different vibe from the mega-clubs of the island's big resorts, this welcoming dance club is dedicated to swing, blues and soul music in Palma's trendy Santa Catalina neighbourhood. Guests can join a swing class, catch a live gig or tuck into some *empanadas* (stuffed pastry).

❹ Vintage Santa Catalina, Palma

MAP C4 ▪ Avda. Argentina, 11 ▪ 634 310272 ▪ Open Mon: 5pm onwards, Tue–Sun: 1pm onwards

Sink into a sofa with a margarita or sit out on the breezy little terrace at this charming café-bar. Its friendly staff, upbeat music, mishmash of vintage furniture and relaxed atmosphere have made this place a favourite in Santa Catalina. As well as some delicious Mediterranean food, the menu features Mexican dishes such as burritos, nachos and tacos.

❺ Casino Mallorca, Porto Pi, Palma

This Las Vegas-style casino and club *(see p106)* is more than just a glitzy gambling destination; there is an excellent restaurant serving first-rate Spanish cuisine and in summer they offer a programme of concerts from classical to jazz.

Slot machines at Casino Mallorca in Porto Pi, Palma

⑨ El Garito, Palma

MAP C4 ■ Dàrsena de Can Barbarà, s/n ■ 971 485644 ■ Open 8pm–4am Wed– Sat ■ Adm ■ www.garito- cafe.com

This large and fashionable club gets going late (it's a cafe-bar in the early evening). DJs play an eclectic mix of music – everything from house to disco classics – and there's also a regular line- up of live bands, mostly from abroad (check the website for all the latest bookings). The fun atmosphere and inexpensive drinks attract a diverse crowd of local and international partygoers all hell-bent on having a good time. It is located a little out of the way, to the west of the city centre, so it's best to take a taxi if you are staying somewhere central.

⑥ Escape Bar, Palma

Something of a local institution, this long-established boho bar (see p98) in Palma is located close to one of the city's prettiest squares. It is open from mid-morning until the early hours, with some customers apparently set on drinking the whole day through. All the staff speak excellent English, and there are several big screens showing major sports events.

⑦ Gaudí, Palma

Plain and straightforward, this popular neighbourhood haunt (see p98) has a graffiti wall and a casual-meets-careworn look. As well as a great selection of cocktails, there's an extensive choice of tapas, pizzas and other snacks to consume either inside or outside on the pavement terrace.

⑧ Jazz Voyeur Club, Palma

MAP K4 ■ C/Apuntadors, 5 ■ 971 720780 ■ www.jazzvoyeur.com
In the midst of the tourist throng, this small but eclectic jazz club features live sounds on most nights. It showcases local musical talent as well as international jazz and blues artists and bands – have a look at the website for details of who's performing and when. Drinks can be pricey, so check the menu carefully before placing your order.

Dancing at Tito's, Palma

⑩ Tito's, Palma

MAP C4 ■ Avda. de Gabriel Roca 31 ■ 971 730017 ■ Open from 11pm Wed–Fri & Sun; from 10pm Sat ■ www.titosmallorca.com
Palma's other huge nightlife venue is popular with a younger crowd. The decor is modern, with lots of stainless steel in evidence, and the light show and sound system are up-to-the- minute. The music ranges from house to Top 40, and Sunday is Gay Night.

📶 Culinary Highlights

Arròs negre with squid and peppers

1 Arròs

Arròs (rice) dishes include the familiar *paella Valenciana*, saffron rice with a mixture of vegetables, chicken and sausage; *arròs brut*, a meaty rice stew; and *arròs negre*, rice with seafood cooked using squid ink.

2 Vi de la Casa

Mallorca is now enjoying a decided upswing in its wine production, and you can generally depend on the house wines being very good. The reds are considered the island's best at the moment, being robust and aromatic, though some whites attain a lively fruitiness.

3 Tumbet

The vegetables that go to make up this *ratatouille*-style stew can vary widely, depending on the season, but it will classically comprise a selection from among the following: aubergine (eggplant), bell peppers, courgettes (zucchini), onions, cabbage and potatoes. The seasoning is mainly garlic.

4 Frit Mallorquí and Llom amb Col

Frit is a hugely popular local dish made with meat offal or fish, cooked in oil with potatoes, onions and vegetables. It is at its savoury best in some of the more traditional market towns of Es Pla. *Llom amb col*, pork wrapped in cabbage, is equally traditional and substantial.

Ensaïmada, a typical Mallorcan sweet

5 Ensaïmades

These unbelievably light and flaky spiral pastries are the pride of the island. Enjoyed any time of day, they can be dusted with icing sugar or filled with candied fruits or jam.

6 Pa amb Oli

This is the most popular Mallorcan (and greater Catalonian) snack – a regional version of the more internationally known bruschetta. The basic item is brown bread rubbed with garlic, then smeared with fresh tomato, drizzled with olive oil and sprinkled with salt. To this basic recipe, anything can be added – usually ham and/or cheese.

Tumbet, **traditionally served in a terracotta dish**

Meat at a butcher's stall in Palma

(7) Pork Sausages

Mallorca's most prized paprika sausage, *sobrassada*, comes from the island's famous small black pigs. It is tender, flavourful and tinged red from spices, and there are various versions of it, including a *sobrassada* pâté for spreading on toast.

(8) Sea Bass Baked in Rock Salt

The Mallorcan version of this classic is the pièce de résistance wherever it is served. The salt pack keeps the moisture and flavour inside, but the delicate, succulent fish is left with a hint of saltiness to add piquancy.

(9) Sopes Mallorquinas

By far the best of Mallorca's *sopes* (soups) is fish soup, a hearty stew of shellfish and white fish in a broth flavoured with garlic and saffron. It may also contain rice or pasta for added body. Other soups common on the island are concoctions of vegetables and mixed meats, often seasoned with garlic.

(10) Canya and Hierbas

Canya is the term for local draught beer, and *hierbas* is a famed herbal liqueur. *Cervesa* (beer) tends to be of the Pilsner type, though in Palma you can find a local variety that is black, fizzy and bitter.

TOP 10 TAPAS TYPES

1 Pickled
The easiest finger-nibbles: olives (sometimes very salty), miniature pickles and possibly pearl onions.

2 Marinated
All manner of seafood, including anchovies, sardines and shellfish, steeped in pale green olive oil.

3 Padrones
These are small green peppers, fried with salt, garlic and olive oil.

4 With Mayonnaise
Patatas bravas, fried potato cubes with mayonnaise and spicy red sauce, are a favourite. As is aïoli, a pungent, but delicious, mix of garlic and mayonnaise.

5 On Bread
The signature bread snack *pa amb oli* is brown bread with olive oil, tomato and other toppings.

6 Egg-Based
Truita espanyol is a potato, egg and onion omelette, served by the slice. *Revuelto de huevos*, scrambled eggs, is popularly served with prawns.

7 Fried
Chipirones and calamari rings are also favourites, along with croquettes.

8 Grilled or Roasted
From snails roasted with garlic to grilled baby squid, octopus, aubergine, kebabs and sweet bell peppers.

9 Stewed or Steamed
As well as *tumbet*, steamed shellfish, broad green beans and artichokes shouldn't be missed.

10 Cured
A cured favourite is salted cod. Sliced cured ham can also be found everywhere, along with the tasty local sausage, *sobrassada*.

Mallorcan *sobrassada* sausages

▣ Cafés

Chic, muted colours in the dining area and bar at the Goli Café

1 **Goli Café, Santanyí**

Set in an old building in the heart of pretty Santanyí, this modern café *(see p123)* serves snacks and meals in the elegant dining room or out on the shaded roof terrace. The creamy walls, exposed brick and beamed ceilings make for a delightful setting to enjoy the generous portions of German and European cuisine on offer.

2 **Café Roma, Palma**

This relaxed, modern café *(see p98)* is located away from the main tourist scrum. The chef serves up authentic Spanish and Mallorcan bocadillos and tapas from as little as €5 (the meatballs are especially tasty). It is open until midnight and is a really popular spot with families.

3 **Sa Pedra, Porto Cristo**

Head to this café *(see p123)* if you want to gaze out at Porto Cristo's lovely harbour and sandy beach while lingering over a drink or fancy ice cream and soaking up the laid-back atmosphere of the town. It is also an ideal listening post for the musical entertainment at the nearby park.

4 **Grand Café Cappuccino**

An elegant 18th-century palace set around a palm-filled patio houses this charming café *(see p98)*. The dining areas have been smartly refurbished, but do not have the appeal of the pretty courtyard with its romantic stone fountain. Drinks, snacks, delicious salads and fresh full meals are served here. There are several

Courtyard, Grand Café Cappuccino

branches of Café Cappuccino in Palma and others located at various points around the island. All of them have good service.

5 Café Sa Plaça, Sineu

At this café-restaurant *(see p130)* in the town's central square, guests can take in a view of the magnificent church of Santa María as they enjoy their meal. On Wednesdays there is the spectacle of the vibrant local market. This café is the place to sample *orxata*, a sweet, creamy soft drink made from water, sugar and tiger nuts (a local plant).

6 Café La Lonja, Palma

At a lovely location near the square, this beautiful, Art Deco-style café *(see p98)* specializes in traditional Mallorcan *garrotines* (grilled baguette-style sandwiches), tapas and drinks. The interiors are eclectic but elegant, and the service is great.

7 Café Scholl, Sóller

This elegant café *(see p105)* with its marble-topped tables and burnished mirrors makes a wonderful spot for a break. Enjoy delicious homemade cake and coffee, or tuck into the tasty quiches or lasagne at lunchtimes. Vegetarians and vegans will find plenty of choices on the menu.

8 Gran Café 1919, Port de Pollença

MAP E1 ■ Passeig d'Anglada Camarassa, 2 ■ 971 868426 ■ Open 8am–9:30pm daily

An ideal corner location on an elegant promenade has been claimed by this old-fashioned café. The staff wear black tie, and the decor evokes belle-époque style with a dash of Catalan Modernista. A wide range of international dishes are available on the menu.

9 Cafè Parisien, Arta

A very inviting spot, this beautiful café *(see p125)* offers fresh and tasty home-cooked dishes (including an excellent set lunch), pastries and coffee. Best of all is the enchanting garden, where guests can linger over drinks and snacks in the shade of olives and vines. The café also regularly hosts live music.

Outdoor seating at Café Sóller

10 Café Sóller, Sóller

This contemporary, relaxed bar and café *(see p105)* serves reasonably priced tapas and pastries. The interior is styled in a novel fashion with colourful modern art and includes giant papier-mâché animals.

🔟 Restaurants

1 Ca Na Toneta, Caimari

Fresh seasonal produce is the key to the outstandingly creative Mallorcan cuisine at this delightful rural restaurant *(see p115)* run by two sisters, Maria and Teresa Solivellas. Much of the produce is grown in their own kitchen garden and the skilful presentation of each dish turns them into miniature works of art.

2 Es Fum, Costa d'en Blanes

This Michelin-starred restaurant *(see p107)* at the St Regis Mardavall Mallorca Resort offers delightful innovative cuisine with impeccable presentation by chef Miguel Navarro. There are two tasting menus from which to choose. With a stunning terrace for alfresco dining, this place is very stylish and popular, so reservations are essential.

3 Adrián Quetglas, Palma

One of the most talked-about chefs on the island, Adrián Quetglas spent a decade in Russia, before returning to Mallorca to open his own restaurant *(see p99)*. A mix of Mediterranean, Russian and Asian flavours influence his creative cuisine, for which he has already received a coveted Michelin star.

4 L'Hermitage, Orient

This restaurant is very off the beaten track, but it's worth the trip for the soaring views and some of Mallorca's very best cuisine. The setting, in a series of elegant medieval rooms and terraces nestled amid lush copses, is also unforgettable. Located in what used to be an olive oil-mill and is now a luxurious hotel *(see p144)*, the restaurant serves creative meals prepared by a top Swedish chef. Dishes such as loin of lamb with dried apricots and a crispy vegetable roll are must-tries, and don't miss the divine desserts.

Dining terrace at Es Fum

Michelin-starred Marc Fosh

5 Marc Fosh, Palma

Situated in the Hotel Convent de la Missió, this stylish gastronomic delight *(see p99)* is run by celebrated chef Marc Fosh. The food on offer is modern Mediterranean fare, and vegetarian options are available. This is a very popular restaurant, so advance reservations are essential.

6 Sebastian, Deià

Housed in a former stable, which is more than 250 years old, this exquisite restaurant *(see p107)* offers a choice of mouth-watering Mediterranean dishes that are created using fresh market produce selected personally by celebrated chef Sebastian Pasch. The lobster ravioli and rack of lamb are old-time favourites. Deià is one of Mallorca's ritziest spots and the restaurant attracts a steady flow of leading celebrities, so booking is pretty much essential.

7 Cuit, Palma

This charming restaurant *(see p99)* in central Palma pairs elegant and assured Mediterranean cuisine with stunning views from its eighth-floor terrace. It is the perfect choice at any time of day, whether coming for the fabulous brunch, a languid lunch, or a romantic dinner. The talented Miquel Calent is a competent helmsman in the kitchen.

8 Miramar, Port d'Alcúdia

Not far from the seafront and centrally located on the promenade, this excellent restaurant *(see p115)* is almost always busy, but the high-quality professional service never suffers. Seafood and fish are the highlights; the fish soup with rice and lobster or the fried lobster with crispy bread are mouth-watering winners. People come here from far and wide, so be sure to reserve ahead.

9 Zaranda, Es Capdellà

The stellar cuisine at Zaranda *(see p107)* is matched only by its heavenly setting at the Castell Son Claret *(see p142)* – if you can, ask for a table on the romantic, lamp-lit terrace. Fernando Pérez Arellano is the only chef with two Michelin stars on the island, and his experimental Mediterranean cuisine and modern cooking techniques continue to delight his guests.

Chic dining room at Zaranda

10 Celler la Parra, Port de Pollença

This long-established, popular restaurant *(see p115)* has been in the same Mallorcan family since 1962. It offers a warm and friendly ambience, great value for money, and delicious fare prepared in a wood-burning oven. Favoured dishes include suckling pig and pork with cabbage. You can eat inside or venture out onto the patio – both are enjoyable.

🔟 Wineries

Examples of Macià Batle wines

1 Bodegas Macià Batle, Santa Maria del Camí

MAP D3 ■ Camí de Coanegra, s/n ■ 971 140014 ■ Open 9am–6:30pm Mon–Sat (check website for tours) ■ Adm ■ www.maciabatle.com

One of the biggest bodegas on the island, this is a stop on the Wine Express tourist train. They produce a range of good wines, which are available for tastings or to buy in the shop. There are regular tours here.

2 Bodegues Ribas, Consell

MAP D3 ■ C/ de Muntanya, 2 ■ 971 622673 ■ Open 10am–6pm Mon–Fri (book tours in advance) ■ www.bodegaribas.com

Established in 1711, the oldest bodega in Mallorca has been with the Ribas family throughout. It is now an organic estate, where they grow many of the island's indigenous grape varieties.

Rows of vines at the Bodegues Ribas

3 Bodegas Can Majoral

MAP D3 ■ Carrero del Campet 6 ■ 971 665867 ■ Open by appt (email celler@canmajoral.com) ■ www.can majoral.com

One of the pre-eminent producers of organic wines in Mallorca, this bodega is passionate about indige-nous grapes such as Prensal, Collet and Gorgollasa. They also host the annual grape harvest at full moon.

4 Bodega Biniagual, Binissalem

This historic wine-producing village has been beautifully restored after a period of neglect, and this small, self-sufficient estate *(see p130)* enjoys an idyllic setting. Once again producing wines in time-honoured tradition, its Veran and Grand Veran wines are par-ticularly good. Book tours in advance.

5 Celler Tianna Negre, Binissalem

MAP D3 ■ Camí des Mitjans ■ 971 886826 ■ www.tiannanegre.com

The striking architecture here reflects the bodega's reputation for being at the vanguard of innovation. Tasting tours can be arranged if booked in advance.

6 Bodega Ramanyà, Santa Maria del Camí

MAP D3 ■ Camí de Coscois ■ 680 417929 ■ www.bodegaramanya.com

Try the unusual cavas from this delightful boutique winery, run by the affable Toni Ramanyà. A visit (advance booking required) includes entry to his superb ethnographical museum, where 2,000 artifacts, including tradi-tional carriages and carts, are housed.

⑦ Bodegas Mesquida Mora, Porreres

MAP E4 ■ Camí de Sant Joan ■ 687 971457 ■ www.mesquidamora.com
The winery is owned by the fourth generation of the Mesquida family. They create biodynamic wines from indigenous and imported grape varieties. Advance booking is required.

Wine barrels, Bodegas Mesquida Mora

⑧ Bodegues Castell Miquel, Alaró

MAP D3 ■ Ctra Alaró-Lloseta km 8.7 ■ 971 510698 ■ Open timings vary (check website) ■ www.castell miquel.com
Phytoneering entrepreneur, Professor Popp has produced some complex wines here. The restored estate's terraces are linked by steep stairways that are illustrated on the wine labels.

⑨ Galmes i Ribot, Santa Margalida

MAP F3 ■ Ctra Santa Margalida-Petra km 2.4 ■ 678 847830 ■ www.galmes iribot.com
The Ribot-Galmés family transformed their estate in 1997, planting vines with the aim of creating top-quality wines. Their bold approach, mixing old vines with new techniques, has paid off.

⑩ Son Prim, Sencelles

MAP D3 ■ Camí de Inca ■ 971 872758 ■ Open by appt (email visit@ sonprim.com) ■ www.sonprim.com
This family-run bodega has gone from strength to strength, producing some superb award-winning wines. They specialize in red wines, with Syrah, Cabernet Sauvignon and Merlot vines, and the local grape Manto Negro.

TOP 10 WINE SHOPS AND DELIS

1 La Vinoteca, Palma
MAP C4 ■ C/Pare Bartomeu Pou, 29 ■ 971 761932
A superb selection of wines from producers across the island.

2 Vera Gastronomia Delicatessen, Pollença
MAP E1 ■ C/Alcúdia, 5 ■ 971 533618
Gourmet goodies, including local Mallorcan specialities, are on sale here.

3 Es Bon Racó, Palma
MAP C4 ■ C/Ausiàs March, 22 ■ 971 498172
This place sells Mallorcan cured meats, cheeses, wines, olive oil and more.

4 Colmado la Montaña, Palma
MAP M3 ■ C/Jaume II, 27 ■ 971 712595
A great shop for *sobrassada*, as well local charcuterie and cheeses.

5 Biogranja La Real, Palma
MAP C3 ■ Camí La Real 5 ■ 971 254195
Great organic fruit and vegetables.

6 Sa Cisterna, Alcúdia
MAP F2 ■ C/Cisterna, 1 ■ 971 548606
A shop with olive oil, wines, local meats and cheeses, plus a bar area to try them.

7 Son Vivot, Palma
MAP P1 ■ Plaça de la Porta Pintada, 1 ■ 971 720748
Specialists in produce from Mallorca and the Balearic islands since 1954.

8 Mallorca Delicatessen Mateu Pons, Palma
MAP N3 ■ Plaça del Marquès del Palmer, 7
A great one-stop shop for a wide range of gourmet goodies from Mallorca.

9 S´Hort de Cartoixa, Valldemossa
MAP C3 ■ C/ de Jovellanos, 6A
Deli offering a selected variety of the best Mallorcan produce.

10 La Pajarita, Palma
MAP L3 ■ C/Sant Nicolau, 2 ■ 971 716986
A charming 19th-century store with a confectionery and a deli.

Confectionery at La Pajarita

🔟 Shopping Places

Glassblower, Gordiola Glassworks

① Gordiola Glassworks

Despite the rather kitsch building in which it is housed, this place *(see p129)* is worth a prolonged visit. Watch the glassblowers engaged in their dangerous art, then spend an hour in the museum upstairs and at least another hour browsing through the vast warehouse shops offering their prodigious output of beautiful glassware.

② Manacor Pearls

The unprepossessing town of Manacor is notable for its manufactured goods, with pride of place going to its world-famous artificial pearls *(see p128)*. The standards of fabrication are exacting, as a free tour of the factory will reveal, along with the variety of shapes and shimmering colours indistinguishable from true pearls.

③ Sa Pobla Market
MAP E2

The town's central square on a Sunday morning is the place to be to see what a real country market is like. Visitors will find the freshest produce – strawberries and potatoes are specialities here – and get to sample the local spicy tapas.

④ Wineries

Top-quality wine production in Mallorca is on the rise, with more and more of the island's vineyards *(see pp82–3)* dedicated to fine wines rather than the table wines for which the island was historically better known. Most bodegas offer tastings and sell their bottles on the premises.

⑤ Inca

Though Inca is a working town, it is the island's centre *(see p130)* for the production of leather goods. Many outlets offer leather jackets, handbags, shoes and a host of other stylish items. The outdoor Thursday market is also well worth a visit.

⑥ Avinguda Jaume III, Palma
MAP K–L3

This elegant, arcaded avenue is one of Palma's main streets for chic boutiques, including Cartier and Loewe and good local shops such as Persepolis for antiques.

⑦ Sant Nicolau and Plaça Major
MAP N3

The pedestrian shopping streets in central Palma form a warren behind Bar Bosch on the main Passeig des Born, with a good selection of shops. In this area, around Plaça Major, there are many speciality gift shops.

Market stall in Palma's Plaça Major

8 El Corte Inglés, Palma
MAP S1; Avda. Alexandre Rosselló, 12; open 9:30am–9:30pm Mon–Sat ∎ MAP K3; Avda. Jaume III, 15; open 9:30am–9:30pm Mon–Sat (11am–8:30pm Sun)

Palma has two branches of Spain's own department store, where the quality and prices are firmly upmarket.

9 Sineu Market
In a historic town in the central plain, this market, held on Wednesdays (see p128), is one of the island's biggest agricultural fairs, where local produce is traded. Pottery, leather and lace are among the goods sold.

Leather bags for sale, Sineu Market

10 Artesanía Textíl Bujosa, Santa Maria del Camí
The festive *robes de llengües* (tongues of flame cloth) are made here (see p130), in every possible colour and design. Watch them being made at this out-of-the-way spot and buy bolts of fabric or ready-made items.

TOP 10 MARKETS

Pottery souvenirs, Sineu Market

1 Palma Daily Markets
Passeig de la Rambla for flowers, Plaça Mayor, Mercado del Olivar, Mercado de Santa Catalina, Mercado de Pere Garau and Mercat de Llevant for produce, and Llotja del Peix for fish.

2 Palma Weekly Markets
Saturday is the day for the vast El Rastro Palmesano Flea Market, on Avda. Alomar Villalonga.

3 Villages on Sunday
A great day for many village markets: Consell, Valldemossa, Santa Maria del Camí, Inca, Sa Pobla, Pollença, Muro, Alcúdia, Porto Cristo, Portocolom, Felanitx and Llucmajor.

4 Villages on Monday
Monday markets are held at Manacor, Montuïri, Caimari, Calvia and Lloret.

5 Villages on Tuesday
Some of the lesser-known villages have markets on Tuesday: Campanet, Alcúdia, Artà, Santa Margalida and Porreres.

6 Villages on Wednesday
A big day for markets, especially at Sineu. Others at Andratx, Selva, Port de Pollença, Capdepera, Petra, Colònia de Sant Jordi and Santanyí.

7 Villages on Thursday
Markets at Inca, as well as Ariany, S'Arenal, Consell, Campos, Ses Salines.

8 Villages on Friday Morning
Inca for leather, Binissalem, for wine, and Son Severa, Llucmajor and Algaida.

9 Villages on Friday Afternoon
Alaró and Can Picafort.

10 Villages on Saturday
This is a very big market day all over the island.

🔟 Mallorca for Free

Detailed tapestry at Palau de l'Almudaina

4 Museo Fundación Juan March, Palma

Set in an elegant 17th-century mansion, this excellent museum (see p96) holds an impressive collection of artworks by some of the most prestigious Spanish artists such as Picasso, Miró and Dalí, and does not charge an entry fee. A number of free workshops and talks are also offered.

1 Palau de l'Almudaina, Palma

The must-visit royal palace (see pp14–15) in central Palma offers free entry to Spanish citizens, residents of the EU and visitors from Ibero-American nations every Wednesday, from 3 to 6pm between October and March and from 5 to 8pm between April and September.

2 Far de Porto Pí, Palma

MAP R2 ■ Ctra Arsenal, 3E ■ 650 438205 ■ www. farsdebalears.org

Sculpture, Fundación Yannick y Ben Jakober

Built in 1617, the Far de Porto Pí, is the third-oldest operational lighthouse in the world and holds a commanding position on Palma's waterfront. The sight was declared a national historic monument in 1983 and has an adjoining museum. Free 90-minute guided tours of the exhibit at the lighthouse are given from Wednesday to Saturday between 10am and 3pm (call or email to book in advance).

3 Ancient Sites

Many of Mallorca's ancient sites (see p42) do not charge visitors an entrance fee, including the Poblat Talaiòtic (Talayotic village) in S'illot, and the necropolis on the Son Real estate.

5 Fundación Yannick y Ben Jakober

This art museum (see p53) has a truly magnificent rural setting, and offers free entry to its famous collection of historic children's portraits (the "Nins"), as well as the beautiful rose gardens and fascinating sculpture garden, on Tuesdays from 2 to 6pm.

6 Castell de Bellver, Palma

This curious, circular castle (see pp16–17), which is one of Palma's most popular attractions, allows visitors to enter for free every Sunday.

Castell de Bellver

Correfoc at a festival in Alaró

⑦ Traditional Festivals

The island's many traditional festivals *(see pp88–9)* offer all kinds of free events. Visitors could watch demons dodge dragons in the popular *correfoc* ("fire-running"), catch some live music, enjoy a fireworks display or battle with Christians.

⑧ CaixaForum Palma

Beautifully set in the Gran Hotel *(see p51)*, a magnificent Modernista building from 1903, this cultural centre offers free access to its permanent exhibition, and hosts a range of free events.

⑨ Local Museums

Entrance is free at many local museums in Mallorca, including the museums in Pollença *(see p52)*, Muro *(see p128)* and Manacor *(see p128)*.

⑩ Nit de l'Art (Art Night), Palma

www.nitdelartartpalma.com

The Nit de l'Art (Art Night) takes place every year on the third Thursday of September, when the galleries and museums of Palma's old quarter host exhibitions, performances, installations and urban interventions. It has become one of the most popular and exciting free art events on the island.

TOP 10 BUDGET TIPS

1 Holiday packages
Fantastic deals can be had on package holidays, especially if dates are flexible. The low season has the best deals.

2 EMT travel pass
www.emtpalma.cat
Ten-ticket bus passes offer better value for those travelling around Palma.

3 Local tourist offices
The local tourist offices in Palma and across the island provide free maps, and lists of free events and activities.

4 Discounts at museums
Most museums offer discounts for children, seniors, students and the unemployed, as long as you can produce valid documentation.

5 Parking
The larger towns of Mallorca have metered street parking with a per-hour rate. Parking is free in the afternoon.

6 VAT refund
Non-EU residents can get the IVA (VAT or sales tax) returned at participating stores for purchases of more than €90.

7 Local festivals
Festivals provide free entertainment and inexpensive food, particularly at the communal street party meals.

8 Picnics
Sunny weather, superb markets and tasty, good-value local produce make this a great destination for picnicking.

9 Menú del día
Set-price lunch menus are usually excellent value, and can also put some of the fanciest restaurants within the reach of limited budgets.

10 Local wines
Mallorca's impressive range of local wines are not only cheaper than comparable wines from elsewhere, but can be a better complement to the food.

Local Mallorcan wine

〚TOP10〛 Festivals

① Revetlla de Sant Antoni Abat
17 Jan ▪ Palma, Sa Pobla, Muro and elsewhere

One of Mallorca's most unusual festivals, in honour of the patron saint of animals. For two days in Sa Pobla, pets are led through the town to be blessed at the church. Elsewhere, dancers drive out costumed devils, and crowds circle bonfires and eat pastries of spinach and marsh eels.

② Festes de Sant Sebastià
Last fortnight in Jan ▪ Palma de Mallorca and Pollença

Palma's patron saint is honoured with fireworks, dragons, processions, street concerts and beach parties in one of the island's most colourful and exuberant festivals.

③ Maundy Thursday
Mar or Apr ▪ Palma

Setmana Santa (Holy Week) in the capital city is observed by a solemn procession of some 5,000 people parading Christian icons.

Maundy Thursday in Palma

Good Friday procession, Pollença

④ Good Friday
Mar or Apr ▪ Pollença and elsewhere

Many Mallorcan towns have processions during Holy Week. The Calvari steps in Pollença are the scene of a moving torch-lit re-enactment, the Davallament (the Lowering) each Good Friday, when, in total silence, a figure of Christ is removed from a cross and carried down the steps.

⑤ Festa de l'Àngel
Sun after Easter

Villages across Mallorca celebrate the Feast Day of the Angel with a pilgrimage to their local shrine. The biggest event takes place in Palma's Castell de Bellver (see pp16–17) but the pilgrimage from Alaró (see p54) to its castle is also very colourful.

⑥ Festa de Nostra Senyora de la Victòria
From 2nd Sun in May ▪ Port de Sóller

Port de Sóller is the venue for a mock battle between Christians and Moors, in commemoration of a skirmish in which Arabic corsairs were routed in 1561. Expect lots of rowdy, boozy fun, brandishing of swords and firing of antique guns.

⑦ Día de Mare de Déu del Carme
15 & 16 Jul ▪ Palma, Port de Sóller, Colònia de Sant Pere, Portocolom, Cala Ratjada & other ports

This celebration of the patron saint of seafarers and fishermen takes place in various coastal settlements. Boats are blessed, torches are lit (as at Port de Sóller), and sailors carry effigies of the Virgin Mary.

⑧ Festa de Sant Jaume
Week leading up to 25 Jul
■ Alcúdia

St James is celebrated with the usual summer revelry, including folk dancing, fireworks and parades featuring an icon of the saint and various religious symbols.

⑨ Mare de Déu dels Àngels
2 Aug ■ Pollença

This long mock battle between the Christians and the Moors takes place in Pollença. The town spends a whole year preparing for the event, at which hundreds of youths dress up.

Fireworks at Festa de Sant Bartomeu

⑩ Festa de Sant Bartomeu
Until 24 Aug ■ Sóller

The highly charged Nit de Foc (Night of Fire) marks the end of a fortnight-long fiesta for Sant Bartomeu, Sóller's patron saint. People dressed as devils with forks and firecrackers playfully chase locals around Plaça Constitució, while pyrotechnicians organize a spectacular smoky atmosphere and fireworks display.

TOP 10 FIGURES IN MALLORCA'S RELIGIOUS HISTORY

1 Lluc
Legend recounts that over 800 years ago a young boy named Lluc discovered the effigy of the Madonna in the mountains and presented it to the nearest monk (see pp30–31).

2 Gaudí
The devout architect was responsible for the restoration of Palma Cathedral and other holy sites on the island.

3 Knights Templar
A rich and powerful brotherhood of Christian military monks had their headquarters in Palma (see p96).

4 Inquisition Judges
The much-hated Inquisition was introduced to the island in 1484 and led to at least 85 people being burned alive between 1484 and 1512.

5 Xuetes
The name given to the Jews who were coerced by the Inquisition into converting to Catholicism.

6 Junípero Serra
An important 18th-century monk, missionary and colonialist, born in the town of Petra (see p127).

7 Santa Catalina
The island's only homegrown saint, Santa Catalina Thomás was born in 1531 in Valldemossa (see pp22–3).

8 Cardinal Despuig
The 18th-century cardinal developed the more opulent side of church life on the island when he built his grand country home, Raixa (see p102).

9 Bishop Campins
The driving force behind the renewal of the monastery at Lluc as a pilgrimage site.

10 Ramon Llull
The 13th-century Mallorcan writer and philosopher founded several religious observances on the island.

Statue of Ramon Llull, Palma

Mallorca
Area by Area

Striking cliffs and rocky
coastline of Cap de Formentor

⁝⁑⁑ Palma

Basílica de Sant Francesc

In 1983, Palma became the capital of the newly created Autonomous Community of the Balearic Islands and transformed itself from a provincial town into a thriving metropolis. Today, it has over 400,000 inhabitants and captivates all visitors as it once captivated Jaume I, who, after conquering it in 1229, is supposed to have described it as the "loveliest town that I have ever seen". It is pleasant to stroll along the clean, attractive streets past renovated historic buildings. The town and harbour are lively, with bars and restaurants busy with locals and tourists.

PALMA

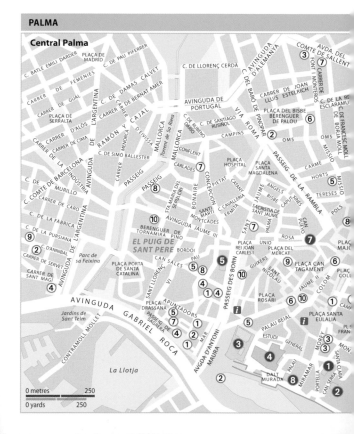

① Museu de Mallorca

MAP N5 ▪ C/de la Portella, 5
▪ 971 177838 ▪ Open 10am–6pm
Tue–Fri, 11am–2pm Sat & Sun ▪ Adm

It is worth the entrance fee just to
see inside the building, a 17th-century
palace built on the foundations of one
of Mallorca's earliest Moorish houses.
The museum *(see p53)* contains some
fascinating exhibits, providing a quick
overview of Mallorca from prehistory
to the 20th century. There are some
powerful recreations of Neolithic
and Bronze Age tombs and dwellings, and several treasures from
the Roman period. Some gorgeous
examples of Modernista furniture
are also on display – in particular,
an interesting console with a
daringly asymmetrical design.

The *tepidarium* at the Banys Àrabs

② Banys Àrabs

MAP N5 ▪ C/Can Serra, 7
▪ 637 046534 ▪ Open 9am–6pm
daily (Apr–Nov: until 7:30pm) ▪ Adm

This 10th-century brick *hammam*
(bathhouse) is one of the few architectural reminders of a Moorish
presence on Mallorca *(see p62)*.
A small chamber has survived
in its original form, with a dome
supported by columns and what
was once underfloor heating. This
would have been the *tepidarium*,
the lukewarm room; there would
have also been a hot room and
a cold plunge.

③ Palau de l'Almudaina

Having been a royal palace
(see pp14–15) for over 1,000 years,
this building's style reflects its long,
fractious history with an uneasy
blending of Moorish and Gothic
elements. Visitors can take a tour
of the palace premises.

Palau de l'Almudaina

The impressive nave and stained-glass windows of La Seu: Palma Cathedral

4 La Seu: Palma Cathedral

Dominating the port, this is the second-largest Gothic cathedral (see pp12–13) in the world and the island's most-visited building.

5 Casal Solleric and Passeig des Born

MAP L3 & L4 ▪ Casal Solleric: open 11am–2pm & 3:30–8:30pm Tue–Sat, 11am–2:30pm Sun & public hols ▪ 971 722092

A splendid Italianate edifice, Casal Solleric was built for a family of olive-oil merchants in 1763 and converted into a modern art gallery in 1995. It stands at the top of the Passeig des Born, which was created in the 19th century on a dried-up riverbed. Similar to Barcelona's famous Ramblas, this is Palma's main promenade and the venue of large-scale cultural events. Set among its plane trees are flowerbeds and seats.

6 Basílica de Sant Francesc

MAP P4 ▪ Plaça Sant Francesc ▪ 971 712695 ▪ Open 10am–6pm Mon–Sat

During the Middle Ages, this was Palma's most fashionable church (see p47), and to be buried here was a major status symbol. Aristocratic families competed with each other by building ever more ostentatious sarcophagi in which to place their dead. The dark interior contains many fine works of art. Next to a 17th-century statue of the Madonna is the carved figure of the medieval writer and philosopher Ramon Llull, who is buried in the church. In front of the basilica is a statue of Junípero Serra, a Franciscan monk, Catholic colonialist and native of Mallorca, who went to California in 1768 and founded Los Angeles and San Francisco.

7 Plaça Weyler

MAP N3

Several interesting examples of Palma's Modernista output are found in this square. The Gran Hotel was Palma's first luxury hotel when it opened in 1903. Designed by eminent Catalan architect Lluís Domènech i Muntaner, it was the building that began the craze for Modernista in the city and is now an excellent free art gallery, CaixaForum, with a permanent display of paintings by Hermen Anglada-Camarasa, and a major venue for temporary exhibitions. Across the street is the wonderful façade of the Fornet de la Soca pastry shop (see p50) next to the old-fashioned Bar Central.

THE HIGHEST-END TOURISM

Although mid-market tourism prevails, plenty of upper-crust visitors make Palma Bay their summer destination. The choicest spot is Port Portals, where King Felipe VI and other royals often berth at the upmarket yacht club. Be aware that prices reflect the jetsetter status of the well-heeled habitués.

8 Museu Diocesà

MAP M5 ■ C/Mirador, 5
■ 971 713133 ■ Open Apr, May &
Oct: 10am–5:15pm Mon–Fri (Jun–
Sep: until 6:15pm; Nov–Mar: until
3:15pm); 10am–2:15pm Sat ■ Adm

The 17th-century Palau Episcopal
houses a little diocesan museum (see
p53). On display are some fascinating
items from Mallorcan churches, and a
selection of majolica tiles. Noteworthy
are a 1468–70 painting of St George
slaying the dragon in front of Palma's
city gate by Pere Nisart; Bishop
Galiana's panel that shows the life of
St Paul (depicted holding a sword); the
Gothic pulpit in a Mudéjar style; and
the sarcophagus of Jaume II, which
stood in the cathedral until 1904. The
palace itself, which is built around a
large courtyard, adjoins the city walls.

**Keep tower,
Castell de Bellver**

9 Castell de Bellver

One of Europe's most
remarkable castles (see pp16–17) was
actually a prison for 700 years and
now houses an excellent museum.

10 Fundació Miró Mallorca

This museum (see pp18–19)
showcases the prolific career of
Catalan artist Joan Miró in all its
depth and variety. It's a highlight
of any trip to Palma.

A WALK AROUND OLD PALMA

> **MID-MORNING**

Start in Plaça Joan Carles I, at
the top of the **Passeig des Born**.
From here, walk east on La Unió
to **Plaça Weyler** to buy pastries at
the Fornet de la Soca (see p50) and
see exhibitions in the Gran Hotel.

Climb the steps to the right of the
Teatre Principal to reach the **Plaça
Major** (see p84). In this beautiful
arcaded square, filled with street
artists and performers, there are
many options to stop for a drink
in one of the cafés.

Come out of the Plaça along
Carrer Sant Miquel. Stop at the
Museu Fundación Juan March
(see p96) and the charming
Església de Sant Miquel.

Now double back through Plaça
Major to view the façades of
L'Aquila and **Can Rei** (see p96). Go
down Carrer Argenteria to visit
the **Església de Santa Eulàlia** (see
p96), and then Carrer Morey to
take in **Ca N'Oleza** (see p96).

LATE MORNING

Continue on to Carrer Miramar,
past the glorious **Palacio Ca Sa
Galesa** hotel (see p142) to exit at
the broad seawall, where you can
look up at **La Seu cathedral**.

Visit the cathedral and **Palau
de l'Almudaina** (see p93), then
go down to the **S'Hort del Rei**
gardens (see p63). Finally, stroll
up the Born and have a snack at
Bar Bosch (Plaça Rei Joan Carles I;
971 712228), or head to one of the
numerous restaurants (see p99)
in the square for a more
substantial lunch.

See map on pp92–3

The Best of the Rest

1 Església de Santa Eulàlia
MAP N4

Built in the mid-1200s in Gothic style, this church *(see p46)* was remodelled in the 19th century and contains a rather elaborate altarpiece.

Nave, Església de Santa Eulàlia

2 Parc de la Mar
MAP M6

The park *(see p63)* next to the cathedral is a popular spot, with a lake, cafés and open-air concerts.

3 Ca N'Oleza
MAP N5 ■ C/Morey, 9

This aristocratic mansion has fabulous wrought-iron railings, a Gothic stairway and graceful balustrades.

4 Sa Llotja
MAP K4 ■ Passeig Sagrera ■ 971 711705 ■ Open 11am–2pm & 5pm–9pm Tue–Sat

This handsome, 15th-century seafront building houses a cultural centre.

5 Fundación Bartolomé March
MAP L4 ■ C/Palau Reial, 18 ■ 971 711122 ■ Open Apr–Oct: 10am–6:30pm Mon–Fri (Nov–Mar: until 5pm), 10am–2pm Sat ■ Adm ■ www.fundacionbmarch.es

The superb sculpture collection at this museum features works by Hepworth, Rodin, Chillida and Moore.

6 L'Aquila/Can Rei
MAP N3

These are two striking examples of Palma's Modernista architecture. L'Aquila combines elements of Catalan Modernista with Viennese tendencies, while Can Rei owes much to the influence of Antonio Gaudí.

7 Can Vivot
MAP N4 ■ C/Can Savellà, 2

Peep in on another of Palma's grand courtyards, with its fine Corinthian columns and elegantly balustraded balcony. Its sumptuous library, filled with a collection of scientific instruments dating from the Enlightenment era, is sometimes open.

8 Museu Fundación Juan March
MAP N3 ■ C/Sant Miquel, 11 ■ 971 710428 ■ Open 10am–6:30pm Mon–Fri, 10:30am–2pm Sat

The collection here includes works by Picasso, Dalí, Miró and Juan Gris.

9 Templar Gate
MAP P5 ■ C/Temple

A fortified gate marks the former entrance to the 13th-century headquarters of the Knights Templar, built when the wealthy brotherhood was in full power. The buildings are now privately owned.

10 Plaça Cort
MAP N4

With its ancient olive tree and elegant façades, including the town hall, this is one of Palma's nicest squares.

Ancient olive tree, Plaça Cort

Shops

Rialto Living, set in a historic mansion with vaulted stone ceilings

① Rialto Living
MAP L4 ■ C/Sant Feliu, 3
■ 971 713331 ■ Open 10am–8pm
Mon–Sat

This ultra-stylish lifestyle store stocks everything from books and fashion to beds and sofas.

② Santa Catalina Market
MAP S1 ■ Plaça Navegació s/n
■ 971 730710 ■ Open 7am–5pm
Mon–Sat

The stalls here are piled with fresh produce, and the café-bars are a great spot for breakfast or tapas.

③ Fine Books
MAP N5 ■ C/d'En Morei, 7 ■ 971
723797 ■ Open 10am–8pm Mon–Sat

A labyrinthine shop full of all manner of used books, mostly in English.

④ Louis Vuitton
MAP L4 ■ Passeig Del Born, 19
■ 971 170890 ■ Open 10:30am–
8:30pm Mon–Sat, 11:30am–6:30pm
Sun ■ es.louisvuitton.com

Upmarket clothes and accessories are sold in an elegant setting here.

⑤ Estilo Sant Feliu
MAP L4 ■ C/de Sant Feliu, 11B
■ 971 425626 ■ Open 10am–8pm
Mon–Sat ■ www.estilosantfeliu.com

A shop selling traditional Mallorcan decorative ceramic and textile goods as well as olive-wood products, many of which are handmade.

⑥ Colmado Santo Domingo
MAP N4 ■ C/S. Domingo, 1
■ 971 714887 ■ Open 10:15am–
7:45pm Mon–Sat

Every foodstuff made on the island is here. Note the impressive array of cured meats strung from the ceiling.

⑦ Alpargateria La Concepción
MAP L2 ■ C/Concepció, 17 ■ 971
710709 ■ Open 10am–1:30pm &
5–8pm Mon–Fri, 10am–1:30pm Sat

This shop sells hand-crafted sandals and espadrilles made on the island.

⑧ Sybilla
MAP L4 ■ C/Sant Feliú, 12
■ 871 038346 ■ Open 10:30am–
8:30pm Mon–Sat

This vast space showcases the celebrated Spanish designer's bold and vivid range of women's fashion.

⑨ Isabel Guarch
MAP M3 ■ Plaça del Mercat, 16
■ 971 284232 ■ Open 10:30am–8pm
Mon–Fri, 10:30am–2pm Sat

A bijou jewellery shop offering unique Mediterranean-inspired pieces designed by Mallorcan Isabel Guarch.

⑩ Bagatela
MAP M4 ■ Passeig del Born, 24
■ 971 715312 ■ Open 11am–8pm
Mon–Fri, 10:30am–1:30pm Sat

This is a one-stop shop for those looking for gifts and crafts.

See map on pp92–3 ←

Cafés and Bars

Exquisite interior of Abaco

1 Abaco
MAP L4 ■ C/Sant Joan, 1 ■ 971 714939 ■ Open 8pm–1am daily (until 2:30am Fri & Sat)

A most romantic setting for drinks: an ancient courtyard and lush garden, with perfumed air and soft candlelight.

2 Café Roma
MAP M1 ■ Baró de Pinopar ■ 971 720321 ■ Open 7am–midnight daily

An unpretentious and inexpensive place popular with locals (see p78). It serves Spanish and Mallorcan cuisine.

3 Ca La Seu
MAP P4 ■ C/Corderia, 17 ■ 660 075511 ■ Open 7–11:45pm Tue–Sat

One of the trendiest spots in the area, this café and bar occupies a former rope and twine shop premises. The tapas are cheap and filling.

4 Grand Café Cappucino
MAP N1 ■ C/Sant Miguel, 53 ■ 971 719764

Since it started operating in the 1990s, this small chain (see p78) has been known for fast service and fresh food.

5 Escape Bar
MAP K4 ■ Plaça Drassana, 13 ■ 971 712916 ■ Open 5pm–1am Mon–Thu, 10am–3am Fri & Sat (until 1am Sun)

Locals and tourists alike have been frequenting this boho bar for many years. It's great for watching sports.

6 Bar Flexas
MAP P3 ■ C/Llotgeta, 12 ■ 971 425938 ■ Open 6:30pm–midnight Tue–Thu (from noon Fri & Sat)

This stylish bar attracts a hip crowd. Its 1940s-style decor is enough to make Franco turn in his grave.

7 Café La Lonja
MAP L4 ■ C/ de la Lonja, 2 ■ 971 722799 ■ Open 10am–1am Mon–Thu (until 2am Fri), 11am–2am Sat (until 1am Sun)

Enjoy lovely views of the historic old town from the patio of this great bar and café (see p78) as you sip on a drink.

8 Ca'n Joan de S'aigo
MAP N3 ■ C/C'an Sanç, 10 ■ 971 710759 ■ Open 8am–9pm daily

Since 1700, this popular Rococo-style café has been serving delicious chocolate, orjata (almond milk), ice cream and pastries. Note that it can get busy.

Drinks with a view at Puro Beach

9 Puro Beach
MAP T2 ■ C/Pagell 1, Cala Estancia ■ 971 744744 ■ Open 11am–7:30pm daily (until 8:30pm Fri & Sat)

A spectacularly situated bar (see p74) that benefits from a cool sea breeze. The DJ plays cool house music.

10 Gaudí
MAP N3 ■ Plaça de la Quartera, 5 ■ 871 704706 ■ Open 9am–11pm Mon–Sat, noon–11pm Sun

Hobnob with some of Palma's most interesting characters at this laid-back café and bar (see p75). The place is popular on weekends, so arrive early.

See map on pp92–3

Places to Eat

PRICE CATEGORIES

For a three-course meal for one with half a bottle of wine (or equivalent meal), taxes and extra charges.

€ under €30 €€ €30–50 €€€ over €50

1 Caballito de Mar
MAP K5 ■ Passeig de Sagrera, 5 ■ 971 721074 ■ Open 1–11:30pm Sun, 1–3:45pm & 7–11:30pm Mon–Thu, 7pm–midnight Fri & Sat ■ €€

One of Palma's top restaurants. Delicious cuisine is on offer, from mango soup to salmon carpaccio.

2 La Bóveda
MAP L5 ■ C/Boteria, 3 ■ 971 714863 ■ Open 1:30–4pm & 8pm–midnight Mon–Sat ■ Closed Feb ■ €€

A charming restaurant in the old fish market. The food is mainly Basque-Castilian, including tapas.

3 Casa Gallega
MAP S1 ■ Avda. del Comte de Sallent, 19 ■ 871 948115 ■ Open 1–4pm & 7:30pm–midnight daily ■ €€

Queue up to enjoy classic Galician cooking here. Options include a *menú del día*, tapas and à la carte.

4 Bon Lloc
MAP K3 ■ C/Sant Feliu, 7 ■ 971 718617 ■ Open 7:30–10:30pm Thu–Sat ■ €€

Palma's best vegan restaurant offers Mediterranean-Asian fusion food.

5 Marc Fosh
MAP N1 ■ C/de la Missió, 7A, ■ 971 720114 ■ Open 1–3pm & 7:30–10pm Mon–Sun ■ €€€

This relaxed restaurant is one of Palma's most popular spots.

6 Celler Sa Premsa
MAP S1 ■ Plaça Bisbe Berenguer de Palou, 8 ■ 971 723529 ■ Open noon–4pm & 7:30–11:30pm Mon–Sat (Jul & Aug: Mon–Fri) ■ €€

Come here for classics such as cabbage rolls with pork, and paella.

7 Tast Club
MAP L2 ■ C/Sant Jaume, 6 ■ 971 710150 ■ Open 1pm–3:30am Mon–Fri, 7pm–3:30am Sat ■ €€

Hidden down a narrow side street off Jaume III, this sophisticated, intimate gem serves up creative tapas and high-quality Mediterranean cuisine.

8 Adrián Quetglas
MAP K2 ■ Passeig Mallorca, 20 ■ 971 781119 ■ Open 1–4pm & 8–11:30pm Tue–Sat ■ €€€

The Michelin-starred eponymous chef creates some of the city's most adventurous contemporary cuisine (see p80). The set tasting menus are superb.

9 Duke Restaurant
MAP S1 ■ Calle Soler, 36 ■ 971 071738 ■ Open 1–4pm & 7:30–11pm Mon–Sat ■ €€

Relaxed and informal, Duke serves healthy international dishes including an excellent three-course menu. It also has a patio for alfresco dining.

10 Cuit
MAP K3 ■ Hotel Nakar, Avda. Jaume III, 21 ■ 871 510046 ■ Open 1–4pm & 7–11pm Mon–Sat; brunch: noon–3pm Sun ■ €€€

The creative cuisine (see p81) is made with the finest local produce and served in a light-filled dining room.

Roof terrace with great views, Cuit

🔟 Southwest Coast

If, as some say, the island's shape suggests a goat facing west, the southwestern coastline makes up his long face while he sniffs the flower petal of Illa Dragonera. In winter, the mountains of this region act as a buffer, shielding the central plain from the fierce *Tramuntana* wind and absorbing most of the island's rain and snow; in summer, they provide a cool retreat, mostly for well-heeled residents and visitors, from the heat of Palma and the south.

Boats in Port de Sóller harbour

① Port de Sóller
MAP C2

This small resort, set around an excellent natural harbour, has vibrant festivals *(see pp88–9)* and the only sandy beach of any size along the western coast. It is the starting point for boat trips along the coast and a good base for walks – there is a short climb to the Cap de Gros lighthouse *(see p57)* with its great views.

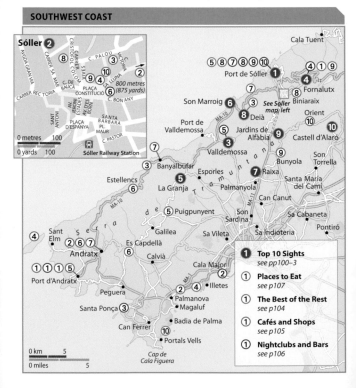

SOUTHWEST COAST

	Top 10 Sights
1	see pp100–3
1	**Places to Eat** see p107
1	**The Best of the Rest** see p104
1	**Cafés and Shops** see p105
1	**Nightclubs and Bars** see p106

Can Prunera art gallery or the Natural History Museum. The town's vintage train provides a superb ride through the mountains to Palma.

③ Valldemossa
MAP C3

It was at the Carthusian monastery in Valldemossa (see pp22–5), one of Mallorca's prettiest hilltop towns, that Polish composer Frédéric Chopin and his lover, writer George Sand, spent one dramatic winter in the early 19th century. The result was Sand's infamous book *A Winter in Majorca*, both a scathing indictment of the island's people and their ways, and a poetic rhapsody in praise of the natural beauties of the town and the island.

④ Fornalutx
MAP D2

This beautiful stone village is wonderfully situated, enjoying a splendid view of towering Puig Major (see p112) – Mallorca's highest peak – and of the steep valley that sweeps down into orchards of orange and lemon groves. Silence reigns, except for the lazy sound of goat and sheep bells. The town seems to cling to its perpendicular foundations, with accommodation and dining options making the most of the panorama. You can get here by car, but a better choice is the fragrant hike up from Sóller, passing through the even tinier Biniaraix (see p104).

Sóller's historic tram to Port de Sóller

② Sóller
MAP C2

The town's name reputedly derives from the Arabic *suliar* – "golden valley" – due to the gorge being famous for its orange groves (see pp28–9). The most notable buildings include Modernista Banco de Sóller, now Santander Bank, and the Neo-Gothic church of Sant Bartomeu, both the work of a disciple of Antoni Gaudí. Sit in Plaça Constitució soaking up the atmosphere, or visit

Fornalutx village, beneath Puig Major

The austere façade of La Granja house, with its colonnaded loggia

5 La Granja
MAP B3

Experience a complete cross-section of traditional Mallorcan life at this noble country estate *(see pp20–21)*.

6 Son Marroig
MAP C2 ■ Ctra de Valldemossa-Deià ■ 971 639158 ■ Open Apr–Oct: 9:30am–8pm Mon–Sat; Nov–Mar: 9:30am–5pm ■ Adm

High above the sea, with its famous Neo-Classical gazebo imported from Italy, this L-shaped mansion was fashioned by Archduke Luis Salvador *(see p24)*. Much admired in Mallorca, the archduke is remembered here with a museum. In the gardens, you can sit in the white Carrara marble rotunda and gaze at the Na Foradada ("pierced rock") Peninsula, jutting out to sea with an 18-m (59-ft) hole at its centre. The mansion has accessible facilities.

Son Marroig gardens

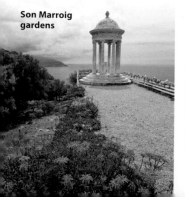

7 Raixa
MAP C3 ■ Palma–Soller road, km 12, Bunyola ■ 971 237636 ■ Open 10am–3pm Tue–Sat

In the 18th century, Mallorcan country homes became a symbol of prestige, and this one, built by Cardinal Antonio Despuig, is one of the finest examples on the island. The cardinal was an antiquarian and so he adorned his Italianate estate with Classical statuary to complement the grand Neo-Classical staircase. The parterres are laid out in the Italian taste of the day, with Classical touches such as fountains and a belvedere, and picturesque medieval references.

8 Deià
MAP C2 ■ La Casa de Robert Graves: open Apr–Oct: 10am–5pm Mon–Fri (until 3pm Sat); Nov–Mar: 9am–4pm (until 2pm Sat) ■ Closed Sun ■ 971 636185 ■ Adm ■ www.lacasaderobert graves.com

Deià *(see p55)* is mostly associated with the English author and poet Robert Graves, who moved here in 1929 and stayed for most of the next 56 years, making the place popular with other writers, such as Alan Sillitoe and Roger McGough, and artists such as Picasso. Graves' house, C'an Alluny, has been turned into a museum of his artifacts and letters. Overlooking the village is the late 15th-century parish church of Sant Joan Baptista, where the writer's grave can be visited. The parish museum is next door, and down the hill is a small museum founded by US archaeologist William Waldren.

⑨ Jardins de Alfàbia

This oasis of heavenly peace high in the mountains was designed by Arab landscape architects 1,000 years ago as an image of Paradise. The gardens *(see p28)* have been reworked over the centuries, mostly with Gothic and Italian Renaissance touches, but the medley of fountains, terraces and groves are still essentially Moorish in style.

Fountains in the Jardins de Alfàbia

⑩ Castell d'Alaró
MAP D3 ▪ 971 940503

The original castle *(see p43)* was built over 1,000 years ago by the Moors and refurbished by Jaume I in the 13th century. It is mostly rubble now, but the lofty position seems unconquerable enough. At the bottom of the trail is Es Vergé, a rustic inn; from here you can follow well-beaten paths along the cliff.

THE FRENCH CONNECTION

Before the Sóller Tunnel opened in 1997, the mountain-ringed Sóller Valley was almost cut off from the rest of the island. Thus, the north of the island carried out more commerce with France than with Palma. Sóller enjoyed a brisk orange trade with France, and their special relationship continues now.

A TOUR OF DRAMATIC PROMONTORIES

▶ MORNING

Start at Andratx *(see p104)* and take the coastal road, the MA-10, north. At the point where the road encounters the coastline is the Mirador de Ricardo Roca viewpoint and the Es Grau café. At **Estellencs** *(see p104)*, there are some good places to stop for shopping and refreshment.

As the road leaves the town and climbs, there is a stopping point to the left, which offers a good look back at the view. Next stop is the magnificent **Mirador de Ses Ànimes** *(see p104)*.

At **Banyalbufar** *(see p104)*, note the remarkable terraced hillsides. A little way on, there are signs for La Granja. Head there for lunch and a good look around the mansion and grounds.

AFTERNOON

After lunch, there is more historic sightseeing to be had at lovely **Valldemossa** *(see p101)*, including the former monastery, modern art museum and the Old Town.

Carrying on north, pop into **Son Marroig** and then wind around into glorious **Deià**, which is a good stop for a stroll.

Continuing on, it can be easy to miss Mallorca's smallest village, Lluc-Alcari. Finally, head for the main square in **Sóller** *(see p101)*, to have a drink at one of the pleasant cafés, then take the quaint tram down to the **Port de Sóller** *(see p100)* for dinner in one of the great fish restaurants lining the harbour.

See map on p100 ←

The Best of the Rest

①Port d'Andratx
MAP A4

This (see p57) is one of Mallorca's classiest seaside resorts.

②Andratx
MAP B4

Surrounded by orange and almond trees, which burst with blossom in February, Andratx is a sleepy place that only becomes animated on market day (Wednesday).

③Mirador de Ses Ànimes
MAP B3

The best mirador (viewpoint) on the entire coast is crowned by the Torre Verger (see p49), which visitors can climb, just as watchmen did for centuries, keeping a fearful eye out for pirates and marauders.

Mirador de Ses Ànimes

④Illa Dragonera
MAP A4

A narrow, rocky island lying at an angle to the coast near Sant Elm, Dragonera has been a nature reserve since 1988 and is home to a wide variety of wild flowers and birdlife, including cormorants, Cory's shear-water and the world's largest colony of Eleonora's falcon. According to legend, the island is visited nightly by dragons. However, its name has more to do with the shape than mythical beasts. A rocky path runs between its two headlands, both marked by lighthouses. Ferries from Sant Elm operate in summer, allowing visitors to explore the island (see p59) for several hours.

⑤Puigpunyent
MAP B3

Lying in the shadow of Puig de Galatzó, this pretty mountain village is the base for visiting the stunning La Reserva nature park (see p68).

⑥Estellencs
MAP B3

This is a tiny, picturesque mountain town (see p54) with restaurants and shops. There is also a rudimentary seaside area around a shingly beach, where the snorkelling is good.

⑦Banyalbufar
MAP B3

Built by the Moors using dry-stone walls, the town's terraces speak of human ingenuity to create superb farmland out of inhospitable cliffs. There are a few nice hotels, some cafés, restaurants and artisan shops, and a small, shingly beach.

⑧Biniaraix
MAP C2

A smaller sibling to Fornalutx (see p101), this charming village clings to the hillside near the Barranc de Biniaraix gorge, offering great views.

⑨Bunyola
MAP C3

This is a pretty place in the foothills of the Serra de Tramuntana. Inside its church is a cherished 14th-century image of the Virgin in alabaster.

⑩Orient
MAP D3

Those who make the hair-raising drive (see p69) from Bunyola to this hamlet at the foot of Puig d'Alfàbia can have a choice of walks, including one to Castell d'Alaró (see p103).

Cafés and Shops

Cappuccino, Port d'Andratx

1 Cappuccino, Port d'Andratx

MAP A4 ▪ Avda. Mateu Bosch, 31 ▪ 971 672214

With a waterfront location by the fishing port, and lovely sunset views, this café serves a range of snacks and coffee, as well as excellent breakfasts. There's also free Wi-Fi.

2 Cooperativa Agrícola Sant Bartomeu, Sóller

MAP C2 ▪ Ctra de Fornalutx, 8 ▪ 971 630294

This cooperative, founded in 1899, produces four delicious types of olive oils: soft Mallorquina, fruity Arbequina, spicy Picual and Coupage (a mix of the three others).

3 Café Scholl, Sóller

MAP D2 ▪ C/Victòria 11 Maig, 9 ▪ 971 632398

Tuck into tasty homemade cakes and sandwiches in this charming, retro-style café (see p79), which also has a small plant-filled terrace. At lunchtime, you can enjoy quiches, moussaka and more, with plenty of choice for vegetarians and vegans.

4 Plaza 13 Couture, Sóller

MAP C2 ▪ Plaça de la Constitució, 13 ▪ 697 434215

Quirky and unusual fashions and accessories for women are elegantly displayed in this stylish shop.

5 Tricia's, Port d'Andratx

MAP A4 ▪ C/Saluet, Local 2 ▪ 971 671922

This glitzy boutique stocks fashion from top international labels, such as Missoni, I love Moschino, and M.i.h. jeans.

6 Ca'n Nadal, Andratx

MAP B4 ▪ C/Juan Carlos I, 7 ▪ 971 236167

Founded in 1872, this pastry shop offers such delights as *mantecados* (shortbread), *cremadillo de cabello* (sugar-coated millefeuille), *pastel de chocolate* (iced chocolate cake with walnuts) or *tortaletta rechesol y frutos secos* (moist tart topped with nuts).

7 Bar Cubano, Andratx

MAP B4 ▪ Plaça Pou, 1 ▪ 971 136367

This bar is where the locals hang out, and it's filled with the usual gambling machines and Mallorcan pottery.

8 Fet a Sóller, Soller

MAP C2 ▪ Plaça des Mercat, s/n ▪ 971 635179

The name means "Made in Sóller" and that is exactly what you get at this gourmet grocery store: locally made jams and marmalades, olive oils, charcuterie, beers, wine, fresh oranges and much more.

9 Café Sóller, Sóller

MAP C2 ▪ Plaça Constitució, 13 ▪ 971 630010

Enjoy modern Mediterranean cuisine at this elegant café. It offers a good mix of vegetarian and meat options.

10 Colmado Sa Lluna, Sóller

MAP C2 ▪ C/Sa Lluna, 3 ▪ 971 630229

Known locally as a mini Fortnum & Mason, this treasure trove offers wonderful Mallorcan wines and foods, as well as great gift ideas.

See map on p100

Nightclubs and Bars

1 Tim's, Port d'Andratx
MAP A4 ▪ Avda. Almirant Riera Alemany ▪ 971 671892

A local institution overlooking the port, Tim's buzzes late into the night. There is live music at weekends and screens for watching sports. The kitchen offers burgers, toasties and other bar fare.

2 Casino Mallorca, Porto Pi, Palma
MAP R2 ▪ Porto Pi Centro Commercial, Avda. Gabriel Roca, 54 ▪ 971 13000

Fix your eyes on the gaming tables here and it's easy to imagine you are in Las Vegas. There are also plenty of glitzy bars and clubby salons for a drink between bets.

3 Scubar, Santa Ponça
MAP B4 ▪ Via Creu, 15 ▪ 622 197423

With blue-and-white decor, this friendly beach bar is an exceptionally relaxed spot to enjoy a post-beach cocktail. It also does simple but tasty snacks, and there are live music performances once a week.

Blue-and-white interior at Scubar

4 Café Sa Plaça, Fornalutx
MAP D2 ▪ C/La Plaça ▪ 971 63 19 21

This is the most popular of the village-square bars, and it is open until late in the summer serving delicious cocktails. There is also live music from 10pm on Sundays.

Pretty façade of Aromas restaurant

5 Aromas, Valldemossa
MAP C3 ▪ C/Rosa, 24 ▪ 685 468004

The plant-filled patio at this charming café is the perfect spot to relax with a glass of wine or a cocktail and a platter of cheeses and charcuterie.

6 Café Central, Sóller
MAP C2 ▪ Plaça Constitució, 32 ▪ 971 630008

A popular café that gets really busy at dawn. A good place to have some late tapas and a cocktail or two.

7 Discoteca Altamar, Port de Sóller
MAP C2 ▪ Corner Es Través and C/Antonio Montis ▪ 971 631205

A small, loud disco for the young crowd. Special fiestas include foam parties and tropical nights.

8 Es Mirall, Port de Sóller
MAP C2 ▪ Camí d'es Far, 21 ▪ 646 844174

With a terrace overlooking the bay, this lively bar offers karaoke nights and live music performances.

9 Bar Albatros, Port de Sóller
MAP C2 ▪ C/Marina, 48 ▪ 971 633214

This is a popular bar with both visitors and locals alike. Ask for canya (a beer on tap).

10 The Asgard, Port de Sóller
MAP C2 ▪ Passeig Es Través, 15 ▪ 971 631535 ▪ Closed Tue

A pleasant Irish pub just metres from the beach, serving real Irish beers. There's a big screen for sports fans.

Places to Eat

1 Es Turó, Fornalutx
MAP D2 ▪ Avda. Arbona Colom,
6 ▪ 971 630808 ▪ Closed Thu ▪ €

This much-loved family-run mountain restaurant serves delicious suckling pig and other traditional home-cooked Mallorcan favourites.

2 Es Fum, Costa d'en Blanes
MAP C4 ▪ C/Palma-Andratx, 19, Costa d'en Blanes ▪ 971 629629 ▪ Closed Nov–Mar ▪ €€€

This great restaurant has a prime location and is set within one of Mallorca's most agreeable resorts.

3 Sebastian, Deià
MAP C2 ▪ C/Felipe Bauzá, Deià ▪ 971 639417 ▪ Closed L & Wed ▪ €€€

Deià is something of a magnet for celebrities, and this restaurant, serving Mediterranean cuisine, is one of their favourite haunts.

4 Meson Ca'n Pedro II, Genova
MAP C4 ▪ Rector Vives, 4 ▪ 971 702162 ▪ €€

This hugely popular place with a friendly vibe has been run by the same family since 1976. It offers a wide choice of Mallorcan dishes, but is famed for its succulent grilled meats.

5 Agapanto, Port de Sóller
MAP C2 ▪ C/Camino del Faro, 2 ▪ 971 633860 ▪ Closed Wed ▪ €€€

Mediterranean food, offered up in a classy environment with great views.

Views from the terrace at Agapanto

PRICE CATEGORIES

For a three-course meal for one with half a bottle of wine (or equivalent meal), taxes and extra charges.
....
€ under €30   €€ €30–50   €€€ over €50

---

6 Zaranda, Es Capdellà
MAP B4 ▪ Castell Son Claret, Ctra Es Capdellà-Galilea km 1.7 ▪ 971 138627 ▪ Closed L, Sun & Mon ▪ €€€

Award-winning chef Fernando Pérez Arellano offers spectacular contemporary Mediterranean cuisine in a truly romantic hilltop setting. This is arguably Mallorca's finest restaurant.

7 Bens d'Avall, Deià
MAP C2 ▪ Urb. Costa Deià, Ctr. Sóller Deià, s/n ▪ 971 632381 ▪ Closed Dec–Mar ▪ €€€

A popular restaurant with stunning mountain and sea views, and memorable Mediterranean and nouvelle cuisine. The menu changes each month to make the most of the season's best produce.

8 Es Canyís, Port de Sóller
MAP A4 ▪ Passeig Platja d'en Repic, 21 ▪ 971 631406 ▪ Closed Mon ▪ €€

Overlooking the seafront, this elegant, family-run restaurant has been serving fresh seafood and local dishes for more than half a century. Save room for the homemade desserts.

9 Ca N'Antuna, Fornalutx
MAP D2 ▪ C/Arbona Colon, 4 ▪ 971 633068 ▪ Closed Mon ▪ €€

Tasty Mallorcan food, with stunning views from the terrace. The paella is also recommended.

10 Wellies, Puerto Portals
MAP B4 ▪ Puerto Portals, 23–4 ▪ 871 902306 ▪ €€€

This friendly, English-owned place with magnificent views over the marina offers imaginative British classics and Mediterranean fare.

See map on p100

🔟 North Coast

The north coast of Mallorca is ruggedly beautiful, with a series of jagged peaks rising high above plunging valleys and steep ravines. For the most part, the mountains shield the ocean, but here and there the coast is interrupted by narrow cove beaches and a string of exceptionally pretty mountain villages. The sheer beauty of the landscape has attracted a large number of international visitors in recent years, though the British have been coming here in large numbers for many years.

Statue at the Monestir de Nostra Senyora de Lluc

1 Gorg Blau
MAP D2

Heading out of Sóller, on the way to Lluc, the MA-10 is perhaps the most dramatic drive of all, traversing tunnels and narrow gorges on its way between Puig Major and Puig Massanella. This beautiful but bleak ravine *(see p58)* has been known since ancient times, as evidenced by the Talayot pillar that has been left as a silent sentinel. Several picturesque man-made reservoirs have been created nearby.

2 Península de Formentor

Mallorca's wildest part *(see pp32–3)* is full of vivid vistas and precipitous plunges, where driving or hiking are exhilarating and unforgettable experiences. It is also home to Mallorca's most venerable hotel, where movie stars have stayed, and where crowned heads and diplomats have decided the fate of nations.

3 Ermita de Nostra Senyora del Puig
MAP E2

As with all of Mallorca's religious retreats, it is the serenity of ageless isolation that rewards visitors here. Though located only a 1-hour walk from atmospheric Pollença, this hermitage *(see p45)* feels a world

NORTH COAST

- 🔟 **Top 10 Sights**
  see pp108–11
- ① **Places to Eat**
  see p115
- ① **The Best of the Rest**
  see p112
- ① **Cafés and Shops**
  see p113
- ① **Nightclubs and Bars**
  see p114

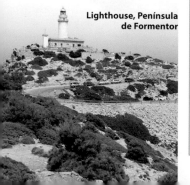

Lighthouse, Península de Formentor

away from modern life, set on this modest bump of a hill barely 300 m (984 ft) high. Over the centuries, the typically tawny-hued stone complex has been home to both nuns and monks, but now, even though it is still church property, only overnight guests use the cubicles. A drystone path leads up the hill, the air filled with the pungent smell of wild herbs. The arid landscape is broken up with olive, carob and fig trees, and dashes of oleander and wild flowers.

Road winding down the hill to Cala Tuent

4 **Son Real**
MAP F3 ■ Ctra Artà-Port d'Alcúdia, km 17 ■ 971 185363 ■ Open 9am–4pm daily
A combination of working farm, nature reserve and necropolis

(see p42), the Son Real estate covers almost 4 sq km (1.5 sq miles). The old restored farm buildings display traditional tools and interiors, and an information centre provides an overview of the area's history. Surrounding the estate is a beautiful nature reserve that is popular with birdwatchers and hikers.

MALLORCA'S HEIGHTS

The Serra de Tramuntana range runs for 88 km (55 miles) from Andratx in the south to Pollença. Its highest peaks, between Sóller and Lluc, are Puig Major (1,447 m/4,747 ft) and Puig Massanella (1,367 m/4,485 ft). Explore the mountains on foot, if possible, to smell wild rosemary, listen to sheep bells, breathe in pure air and marvel at pine trees growing out of red rocks.

Alcúdia and Port d'Alcúdia

This two-part municipality consists of Mallorca's most striking medieval town (see pp34–5), uneasily conjoined with one of its brashest tourist ports (see p57). The area around the fishing harbour is the most attractive, with broad promenade of Passeig Marítim facing a row of shops and some excellent fish restaurants.

Cala Sant Vicenç
MAP E1

The resort has possibly the clearest, most beautiful blue waters of any truly sandy beach on the island, yet is rarely over-crowded. There are actually three *calas* (coves), Cala Sant Vicenç (see p60), Cala Barques and Cala Molins, separated by the Punta de Torre rocky outcrop. Cala Molins is accessed down a steep hill from the main part of the resort and has the most laid-back character, as well as a broader beach and better facilities than the others.

Port de Pollença
MAP E1

This port is a major resort (see p56), with beautiful restaurants, unique shops, a lovely pedestrian-only zone right along the water and bags of nightlife. It is a favourite with families year-round, while older visitors flock there during the winter months. A large community of foreign residents, mostly retired British nationals, has made Port de Pollença a permanent home.

Osprey, Parc Natural de S'Albufera

Parc Natural de S'Albufera
MAP F2

The wetland south of Port d'Alcúdia was once a swamp, most of which was drained in the 1860s. The remaining marshes, overgrown with reeds, can be explored via marked trails. A major conservation project, this is an excellent place (see p59) for bird-watching.

Pollença
MAP E1

Founded by the Romans in the foothills of the Serra de Tramuntana, Pollença still has much of its old-world charm with narrow, twisting streets, some good restaurants and

Cala Molins beach at Cala Sant Vicenç

A quiet street in Pollença

a lively Sunday market. There is a great municipal museum (see p52) too, while the pride of the town is the beautiful Way of the Cross, leading to a chapel that houses a Gothic statue of Christ. There is a seemingly endless set of steps (365 in all) that climb past the Stations of the Cross, leading to the chapel. The statue is carried around town on Good Friday, in a moving torchlight procession (see p88).

10 Monestir de Nostra Senyora de Lluc

Long before the existence of Christianity, this spot (see pp30–31) was Mallorca's holiest pilgrimage point. The heady mountain air and the presence of many groves of oak trees, considered sacred in Neolithic and ancient cultures, combine to create a peaceful, inviting atmosphere for believers and non-believers alike. Visitors can arrange to stay in the monastery's comfortable rooms and can explore the many ancient mysteries of the surrounding area.

A STROLL AROUND HISTORIC POLLENÇA

▶ MID-MORNING

Beginning at about 10am, on any day but Monday, this walk around **Pollença** should take 3 to 4 hours.

Start on the southern side of town, with a visit to the **Museu Municipal de Pollença** (see p52) and the beautiful building that houses it – the convent, church and cloister of Sant Domingo are now given over to civic cultural purposes (closed on Mondays).

Walk north a couple of blocks and continue up to the Plaça Mayor and admire the Modernista architecture of the Hotel Juma and the marvellous rose window tracery of **Nostra Senyora dels Àngels** (see p46) parish church. Nearby store **Nilay** (C/ del Sindical 54), selling handmade items, is worth a visit.

EARLY AFTERNOON

Now walk up the left-hand side of the church along Carrer Monti-Sion to **Ceràmiques Monti-Sion** (see p113), a traditional ceramics workshop. Heading along Carrer d'Antoni Maura, stop at **Café-Bar Juma** (see p113) for some refreshments before striding up the famous Calvari steps.

Finally, head down Les Creus and Gruat streets to the picturesque Pont Romà, a bridge thought by some to be from ancient Roman times, but probably dating from the Middle Ages.

Finish the morning with lunch at **Es Cantonet** (see p125) or the popular **Celler la Parra** (see p81).

See map on pp108–9 ←

The Best of the Rest

1 Mirador de Ses Barques
MAP D2

Located above Sóller, on the road to Sa Calobra, this marvellous viewpoint overlooks the skein of road loops, and, beyond all of the rocky outcroppings, the sea. Stop for refreshment at the restaurant here.

2 Sa Calobra
A rapturously beautiful bay (see p68), which explains why the tourist buses pour in by the dozen every day. The drive via the steep, winding road is also memorable. An easier approach is by boat from Port de Sóller, passing isolated bays and with great views of Puig Major.

3 Torrent de Pareis
MAP D2

There is a walk through a tunnel from Sa Calobra to reach the Torrent de Pareis, which begins in the mountains at the confluence of the torrents of Lluc and Gorg. This canyon (see p58) is the second largest in the Mediterranean, and the point at which it emerges into the sea is spectacular. However, hiking in the canyon can be dangerous, especially after rain.

4 Puig Major
MAP D2

Jutting skyward like an enormous stony crown, this majestic mountain rises up from the landscape. It is flanked on one side by the Sóller Valley, with its picturesque villages, and on the other by Lluc (see p110) and the tranquil valley of Aubarca.

The rocky peak of Puig Major

5 Castell del Rei
MAP E1 ▪ 971 530801 ▪ Walk by prior request only

A popular walk leads to this remote, abandoned mountain castle (see p43) north of Pollença.

6 Cala Tuent
MAP D2

A small cove with 13th-century church Ermita de Sant Llorenç (see pp44–5), Cala Tuent (see p61) is probably the quietest beach on the north coast.

7 Santuari Ermita de la Victòria
MAP F1

Built in 1678, the church is as much a fortress as a spiritual centre due to pirate raids in that era. It houses a revered icon and a vibrant altarpiece.

8 Cap des Pinar
MAP F1

Much of the cape is a restricted military zone, but you can take in the view from the terrace of the Mirador del Victòria, walk to the ruins of the Talaia d'Alcúdia or climb Penya Roja.

9 Coves de Campanet
MAP E2 ▪ C713, 16 km (10 miles) SW of Alcúdia ▪ 971 516130 ▪ Open Apr–Sep: 10am–6:30pm; Oct–Mar: 10am–5:30pm ▪ Adm

The tour of this cave complex with a lake lasts 45 minutes and is less crowded than others.

10 Mirador de Mal Pas
MAP F1

This viewpoint is the first stop on the Península de Formentor (see pp32–3).

Cafés and Shops

1 Café-Bar Juma, Pollença
MAP E1 ▪ Plaça Major, 9 ▪ 971 535002

Overlooking the main square, this is a popular place for a drink and a selection of tapas. Try the tasty meatballs in tomato sauce.

2 Bar Mallorca, Cala Sant Vicenç
MAP E1 ▪ Cala Molins ▪ 971 534603

On the beach, look for the little stone hut with a red-tile roof and with dried grasses over its terrace. It is open late for drinks and snacks.

3 Multi-Hire, Pollença
MAP E1 ▪ Calle Mendéz Nuñéz, 21 ▪ 971 864080

This place offers everything visitors may need to rent on holiday, including bikes for all ages, mobility scooters, baby equipment and air-conditioning units. Food hampers can also be delivered to your accommodation.

4 Ceràmiques Monti-Sion, Pollença
MAP E1 ▪ C/Monti-Sion, 19 ▪ 971 533500

A traditional ceramics workshop with beautiful reproduction tiles and antique originals dating from the 18th and 19th centuries.

5 Rustic Café, Port de Pollença
MAP E1 ▪ Ctra Formentor, 114 ▪ 640 559591

A friendly and laid-back café-bar overlooking the seafront, this has an eclectic menu featuring everything from classic Spanish tapas to Indian samosas and curries. It is part of the popular Pollença tapas route.

6 Galeries Vicenç, Pollença
MAP E1 ▪ Can Berenguer Roundabout (Rotonda) ▪ 971 530450 ▪ www.teixitsvicens.com

Two large floors full of Mallorcan crafts and original art are filled with traditional *robes de llengües* cloth, genuine antiques, lamps, sculpture, rustic furniture, wooden bowls, ceramics and glassware.

7 Helados Garrido, Port d'Alcúdia
MAP F2 ▪ Passeig Marítim, 32 ▪ 971 548290

This traditional café by the port has a wide range of ice-cream flavours to choose from, along with crêpes and classic ice-cream desserts.

8 Uplaça, Pollença
MAP E1 ▪ Plaça Mayor, 4 ▪ 971 876206

Tuck into tasty local tapas, including fried calamari or freshly grilled squid, out on the terrace, which enjoys a prime position on the main square.

Ceramic items on display in Arrels

9 Arrels, Port de Pollença
MAP E1 ▪ Passeig Saralegui, 54 ▪ 971 867017

Some of the island's best handmade Mallorcan crafts are stocked here. The traditional ceramic whistles are featured, as well as fine olive-wood carvings and a special line of leather masks by Calimba of Palma.

10 Cafè de Sa Plaça, Alcúdia
MAP F2 ▪ Plaça de la Constitució ▪ 971 548793 ▪ Closed Jan–Mar

A rustic place with a shady terrace overlooking the square, this café is ideal for a drink and some tapas, or perhaps some tea and cake.

See map on pp108–9

Nightclubs and Bars

1 La Birreria, Pollença
MAP E1 ■ C/Temple, 7 ■ 696 602718

A veritable temple to beers, this bar has a local and international range of artisan beers, including a guest selection that changes each week. They also offer delicious tapas.

2 Mombasa Café, Port de Pollença
MAP E1 ■ Passeig Saralegui, 130 ■ 971 865831

Fabulous sea views accompany the cocktails at this convivial beachfront bar, which has a terrace (featuring swinging seats) and a cozy interior.

3 Twister, Port d'Alcúdia
MAP F2 ■ Ctra d'Artà, 52 ■ 656 231 964

A good spot for a post-beach drink, this place attracts a lively crowd, and also offers an all-day menu of pub food. It is relaxed early on, but gets busier as the night wears on, and there are regular party nights during the summer season.

4 Skau Disco, Can Picafort
MAP F2 ■ Avda. José Trias, 14 ■ 971 850040 ■ Closed winter: Mon–Fri

One of the oldest discos in Mallorca, Skau was founded in the 1960s. It is famous for its foam parties.

5 Chivas, Port de Pollença
MAP E1 ■ C/Metge Llopis, 1 ■ 971 864820 ■ Closed Nov–Apr: Sun–Thu ■ Adm

The crowd is young, and the place is loud and dark, featuring mirrors and a glass ceiling with a state-of-the-art lighting system.

6 The Lemon Lounge
MAP F1 ■ Atilio Boveri 2 ■ 971 866250

This elegant, open-air bar is a great place to relax with a cocktail. There is also live music in the evenings.

7 Miama Beach Club, Platja de Muro
MAP F2 ■ Avda. del Mar, 8C ■ 637 562416

Laze around on the sun loungers at this chic beach club, or linger over cocktails on the terrace before the crowds pack in for the DJ at night. Tapas and dinners are also served.

8 Menta, Port d'Alcúdia
MAP F2 ■ Avda. Tucan ■ 664 435717 ■ Adm

Done up like a lavish Roman villa, with terraces, fountains and even a swimming pool, Menta is one of the most popular clubs in Mallorca.

9 Shamrock, Port d'Alcúdia
MAP F2 ■ C/Torreta, 3 ■ 971 546665

A busy Irish pub located in the port, Shamrock holds varied live music events every night, and is also a good place to watch sports on TV.

10 Banana Club, Port d'Alcúdia
MAP F2 ■ Avda. Tucan, 1 ■ 971 891023

Topped with an unmissable glass pyramid, this is one of the most popular clubs on Mallorca's northern coast. It attracts both locals and tourists thanks to its great line up of resident and guest DJs, and it hosts a number of different theme nights (including foam parties).

Acrobat show at the Banana Club

Places to Eat

1 Stay, Port de Pollença
MAP E1 ■ Main jetty ■ 971 864013 ■ €€

Fish is the speciality at this excellent upmarket restaurant, but the menu of international fare is huge. The lunch menu is great value.

Smart and bright interior at Stay

2 Bellaverde, Port de Pollença
MAP E1 ■ C/Monges, 14 ■ 675 602528 ■ Closed Mon ■ €€

This outstanding vegetarian and vegan restaurant has a lovely shaded courtyard and a superb menu. Dishes include a delicious pumpkin lasagne.

3 Como en Casa
MAP F2 ■ C/ dels Pins, 4 ■ 971 549033 ■ Closed Mon, L ■ €€

Try the fresh, homemade salads on offer at this restaurant.

4 Pollentia Mar
MAP E1 ■ Via Pollentia, 19 ■ 971 530632 ■ Closed D Sun–Thu; L Fri & Sat ■ €

A wonderful seafood restaurant that specializes in traditional cuisine.

5 Il Giardino, Pollença
MAP E1 ■ Plaça Major, 11 ■ 971 534302 ■ Closed Nov–mid-Apr & Mon ■ €€

One of Pollença's best restaurants, this bistro offers delicious Italian dishes made with fresh, locally sourced produce.

PRICE CATEGORIES

For a three-course meal for one with half a bottle of wine (or equivalent meal), taxes and extra charges.

€ under €30   €€ €30–50   €€€ over €50

6 Ca'n Cuarassa, Port de Pollença
MAP E1 ■ Platja Ca'n Cuarassa ■ 971 864266 ■ €€

Set in a large, handsomely restored mansion with extensive gardens, this restaurant offers both Mallorcan and international specialities including succulent meats grilled over charcoal.

7 Q11
MAP E1 ■ C/ d'Antoni Maura, 11 ■ 971 530239 ■ €

Enjoy modern Mediterranean cuisine in a wonderful setting at this restaurant. Good vegetarian options are also available.

8 Celler la Parra, Port de Pollença
MAP E1 ■ C/Joan XXIII, 84 ■ 971 865041 ■ Closed Mon ■ €€€

A welcoming, traditional restaurant. The decor here is a reminder of quieter island times, but the food and wine is really first-rate.

9 Miramar, Port d'Alcúdia
MAP F2 ■ Passeig Marítim, 2 ■ 971 545293 ■ €€

You are spoilt for choice when it comes to restaurants in Port d'Alcúdia, but this restaurant is one of the best. The speciality is seafood, but there is a good range of Mediterranean dishes to suit most tastes.

10 Ca Na Toneta, Pollença
MAP E1 ■ C/s'Hortizó 21 ■ 971 515226 ■ Closed Jul–Sep: L Mon–Fri; Oct–Jun: Mon–Thu ■ €€€

This enchanting country restaurant (see p80) prepares delicious Mallorcan and Mediterranean cuisine prepared with locally sourced produce.

See map on pp108–9

TOP 10 Southeast Coast

While some of the beaches have seen the worst of the effects of mass tourism, more remain as beautiful as ever, offering some of the Mediterranean's most clear, azure and inviting waters. Here, too, is the verdant Serra de Llevant mountain range and some of the island's best natural parks, not to mention its most important ancient sites and magical caves waiting to be explored.

Boats moored off Cala S'Amarador, part of Parc Natural de Mondragó

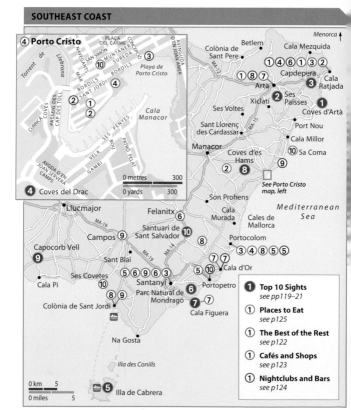

SOUTHEAST COAST

1 **Top 10 Sights**
see pp119–21

1 **Places to Eat**
see p125

1 **The Best of the Rest**
see p122

1 **Cafés and Shops**
see p123

1 **Nightclubs and Bars**
see p124

Previous pages Idyllic view of the Canyamel coast

1 Coves d'Artà
MAP H3 ■ Ctra de las Cuevas, Capdepera ■ 971 841293 ■ Open 10am–5pm daily (May–Oct: until 6pm) ■ Adm

During the Christian Conquest, Jaume I found 2,000 Moors hiding with their cattle in this unusual network of caves. However, it was not until 1876, when speleologist Edouard Martel entered the grottoes, 46 m (151 ft) above the sea at Cap Vermell, that they were studied. Another early visitor was Jules Verne, whose book *Journey to the Centre of the Earth* is said to have been inspired by them.

2 Ses Païsses
MAP G3 ■ South of Artà ■ 619 070010 ■ Open Apr–Oct: 10am–5pm Mon–Sat ■ Adm

A link with the Mallorcans of some 3,000 years ago, these Bronze Age ruins *(see p42)* of a Talayot village include a massive Cyclopean portal formed from three stone slabs weighing up to eight tons each. Inside are several rooms and a watchtower, and the settlement is surrounded by a dry-stone wall.

3 Capdepera
MAP H3

This castle *(see p49)* can be seen from miles away. Its crenellated form sprawling appealingly around the

Capdepera castle above the town

crest of its sizable hill. A citadel of some sort has existed here since Roman times, guarding the sea approach from the east, but the present crenellated classic dates back to King Sanç in the 14th century. It is possible to drive up, though it can be difficult to find the right street in the tightly knit little town below. The walk up from pleasant Plaça de l'Orient is a much better option. Within the walls is a curious little Gothic church that offers some spectacular views from its flat roof.

4 Coves del Drac
Mallorca's most spectacular cave system *(see pp36–7)* can be toured in a gondola-style boat. The experience is enhanced by live music.

The beautifully lit Coves del Drac, with their crystal-clear underground lakes

5 Illa de Cabrera

MAP H6 ■ Park information office: Plaça Espanya, Palma; 971 656282 ■ Boat excursions: C/Explanada del Port, Colònia de Sant Jordi; 622 574806; excursions daily at 9:30am; adm

Cabrera ("Goat Island") lies 18 km (11 miles) off the mainland. A virtually uninhabited place, it nevertheless has a rich history. It served as a prison camp during the Napoleonic War and was used as a base by Barbary pirates. Boat trips leave from Colònia de Sant Jordi and take a day – highlights include a 14th-century castle (see p49) on the island and Cova Blava (see p60). Keep an eye out for the rare Lilford's lizard, identifiable by its dog-like face.

The castle on Illa de Cabrera

6 Parc Natural de Mondragó

MAP F6 ■ South of Portopetro ■ Visitor Centre, Ses Fonts den'Alis: 971 181469

Marked as a protected area in 1992, the park (see p58) incorporates dunes, marshes, rocky coasts, beaches, pine forest, farmland and scrub. Country lanes and easy trails provide access. Look out for herons, egrets, puffins, coots, finches and rabbits.

CONTAINING MASS TOURISM

Mass tourism is now confined to parts of the island where it encroached in the 1960s, primarily Cala Millor and some of the Cales de Mallorca. Other areas, most notably the prototype Cala d'Or, have been developed in a more sensitive way, favouring local styles.

Pretty hamlet of Cala Figuera

7 Cala Figuera

MAP F6

This tiny old fishing hamlet is an underdeveloped gem. It probably owes its survival to the simple fact that it has no beach, the closest one being 4 km (2 miles) away at Cala Santanyí. What it does have is a collection of pleasant low-rise structures and an array of eateries and people-watching cafés. The fishing harbour is part of a fjordlike bay.

8 Coves d'es Hams

These caves (see p37) are less striking than the Coves del Drac or Coves d'Artà. The name Hams means "fish-hooks", which the stalactites are said to resemble. Visitors get a guided tour and a concert.

9 Capocorb Vell

MAP D5 ■ Ctra MA–6014 Llucmajor–Cap Blanc, km 23 ■ 971 180155 ■ Open 10am–5pm Fri–Wed

This ancient Talayot settlement (see p43) was probably established around 1000 BC. Originally, it consisted of five stone structures (talayots) and 28 smaller dwellings. The amazing Cyclopean walls, reaching 4 m (13 ft) in places, would have served as protection, but little more is known about the function of the rooms or the lives of the ancient inhabitants.

FIVE SEASIDE BEAUTIES

Porto Cristo

Cales de Mallorca

Portocolom

Portopetro

Colònia de Sant Jordi

Cala Figuera

Cap de ses Salines

Mediterranean Sea

Be sure to have a drink at the visitors' bar, which would not look out of place in *The Flintstones*.

⑩ Santuari de Sant Salvador

MAP F5 ▪ Ctra de Portocolon, s/n, Felanitx ▪ 971 580056

The castle-like structure is 4 km (2 miles) east of Felanitx, on Puig Sant Salvador, the highest mountain of the Serres de Llevant. Founded in the 14th century, and remodelled in the 18th century, the sanctuary (see p147) is an important place of pilgrimage. As in other former monasteries, visitors can stay in basic rooms.

Santuari de Sant Salvador

▶ MORNING

This itinerary, with driving and walking, will take a full day.

Set out in the morning to lovely **Porto Cristo** (see p122), with its terrace café-restaurants that look over the picturesque port. Pop into **GCH 1991** (see p123), a local boutique selling women's fashion.

Bypassing the infamously overdeveloped Cales de Mallorca, **Portocolom** (see p122) is next, perhaps the most unspoiled and seductively beautiful fishing village left on the island. Be sure to check out the painted façades of the old town, and walk along the waterfront to **Celler Sa Sinia** (see p125) for a delicious seafood lunch while enjoying the stunning views over the harbour.

AFTERNOON

Make your way down to pretty **Portopetro** (see p57), a minus-cule port that has lost none of its authenticity. Have a drink at **Ca'n Martina** (see p125), a restaurant that is in a beautiful setting overlooking the bay.

Pretty **Cala Figuera** is further south. Stroll around its woods-encircled harbour and browse around the gift shops.

On the western side of the Cap de ses Salines is Colònia de Sant Jordi, a popular beach town with a bright, relaxing port. Stop here to have a fresh fish dinner at **Port Blau** (see p125), and spend the night at **Hostal Playa** (see p145).

See map on p118 ←

The Best of the Rest

1 Artà
MAP G3

An ancient, prosperous town, Artà is best known for its basketry.

2 Cala Ratjada
MAP H3

Surrounded by fine beaches and pretty coves, this fishing port (see p57) on Mallorca's eastern tip is a busy resort in summer.

3 Santanyí
MAP F6

This is the café centre for all the expats who own villas nearby, but it is still very Spanish. Buildings are made from the same golden sandstone used in Palma's Cathedral. The streets near the church are the focus of a lively Wednesday market.

Wickerwork from Santanyí market

4 Porto Cristo
MAP G4

Located at the end of a sheltered inlet, Porto Cristo is a family resort. The nearby Coves del Drac and Coves d'es Hams (see pp36–7) are popular with day-trippers.

5 Portocolom
MAP G5

This attractive fishing village was named in honour of Christopher Columbus, who is said (without much evidence) to have been born here. It has found a new lease of life as a resort favoured by the Spanish.

The seafront in Portocolom

6 Felanitx
MAP F5

The town is at the centre of a wine-producing area and also known for its floral-decorated pottery and its capers, or "green pearls", which are on sale at the Sunday market.

7 Cala d'Or
MAP F5

Not just one cove, but many – each with their respective beaches and pueblo-style villas – make up this stylish area. Each former humble fishing dock has metamorphosed into a classy marina catering for a discerning set.

8 Castell de Santuari
MAP G3

Artà's crowning glory is its hilltop fortress, the view from which is Mallorca's most characteristic sight: a jumble of tiles in every shade of brown.

9 Campos
MAP E5

A famous painting by 17th-century Sevillian artist Murillo hangs in the parish church of this dusty agricultural town. Next door is a museum with a collection of offertory bowls.

10 Ses Covetes
MAP E6

There is no trace of the "small caves", presumed ancient Roman burial niches, that inspired the name of this town. Located at the northern end of Es Trenc (see p61), this place has a great beach and a few cafés.

Cafés and Shops

1 **Bar Marítimo, Cala Ratjada**
MAP H3 ▪ Passeig Marítim ▪ 971 738192

A place to relax, have a drink or a snack, and survey the busy boats going in and out, Marítimo looks a bit like the deck of an ocean liner.

2 **Sa Pedra, Porto Cristo**
MAP G4 ▪ C/Verí, 4 ▪ 971 820932 ▪ Closed Tue

Overlooking the palisades, boats and port, this café-restaurant *(see p78)* is hung with contemporary paintings and has a huge terrace. Ice creams, snacks and full meals are available.

3 **Café 3, Cala Ratjada**
MAP H3 ▪ Avda. America, s/n ▪ 971 565356

With views over the marina, this light and airy bar has balconies and spacious, decked outdoor areas, giving it a beach-house feel. During the summer months, there is live music on Tuesday and Friday nights.

4 **Caféteria Chambi, Porto Cristo**
MAP G4 ▪ San Jordi, 4 ▪ 971 820787

Offering modern Mediterranean food, this café has great tapas, as well as a wide variety of vegetarian options.

5 **Sa Plaça, Santanyí**
MAP F6 ▪ Plaça Major, 26 ▪ 971 653278

Come for *pa amb oli (see p76)*, olives, ham, pickled peppers and Mallorcan cheeses. The refurbished interior has marble tabletops and archways, and outside there is plenty of local action in the main square.

6 **Mandala Shoes, Santanyí**
MAP F6 ▪ C/Bisbe Verger, 34 ▪ 606 328247 ▪ Open 10am–2pm & 4:30pm–7:30pm Mon, Tue, Thu & Fri; 10am–2pm Wed & Sat

An exclusive shop for quality leather shoes. Golf shoes are a speciality here. Tailor-made products also available.

7 **Basketry Shops, Artà**
Miguel Fuster: MAP G3; C/Pep Not, 16

Artà town is famous as Mallorca's centre for handsome everyday items made from the tough fibres of the *palmito* (palmetto) plant, which grows wild all over the island.

8 **Panaderia Pons, Colònia de Sant Jordi**
MAP E6 ▪ C/Major, 20 ▪ 971 655171

The *ensaimades* (spiral-shaped sweet pastries) from here are light and fluffy and are sold alongside other delicious local pastries and various picnic essentials.

Goli Café in the evening

9 **Goli Café, Santanyí**
MAP F6 ▪ C/Portell, 14 ▪ 663 499566 ▪ Closed Sun

With beamed ceilings and exposed brick walls, this café *(see p78)* offers good breakfasts and international cuisine. There is also a patio and a roof terrace for alfresco meals.

10 **GCH 1991, Porto Cristo**
MAP G4 ▪ C/Puerto, 7 ▪ 971 821641

This boutique offers a range of dresses, jeans, jackets and evening wear for stylish women, along with a small but highly desirable selection of shoes and accessories. It also has a good choice of beach cover-ups.

See map on p118

Nightclubs and Bars

① Physical, Cala Ratjada
MAP H3 ▪ C/Coconar, 17 ▪ 971 565200

The port attracts a young, active crowd for whom this is the best club in town, leading the way with techno, hip-hop and dance music.

② Twist, Porto Cristo
MAP G4 ▪ Es Riuet ▪ 971 820173

A hip place done up in primary colours, with tiny halogen lights above a granite bar and work by Basque artist S'Anto Iñorrieta.

③ Flamingo, Porto Cristo
MAP G4 ▪ C/Bordils ▪ 971 822259

Offering delicious homemade paellas and seafood, this bar and restaurant has unusual decor that includes cartoons decorated on walls. Outside, the views from the terrace are superb.

④ Noah's Café, Cala Ratjada
MAP H3 ▪ Avda. América, 1–2 ▪ 971 818125

Located on the harbour, with pretty views, Noah's serves healthy food from early in the morning, and very good cocktails until late at night. A relaxed atmosphere and great music. Full access for guests with specific needs.

⑤ Café Chill Out La Playa, Portocolom
MAP G5 ▪ Portocolom beach

A cool and relaxing terrace-bar by the beach with, as the name suggests, a chilled-out vibe. International DJs play Nu Jazz here most evenings.

⑥ Bolero Angels Disco, Cala Ratjada
MAP H3 ▪ C/Leonor Servera, 36 ▪ 971 563490

This glamorously appointed disco is right in the heart of Cala Ratjada. DJs play pop and dance music to the young crowd, and there is live music most nights of the week as well.

⑦ Cala Gran Cocktail Bar, Santanyí
Avda. Blvd D'or, 4 ▪ 871 200658

Located in the centre of town, this welcoming cocktail bar has great drinks and an amazing terrace. It offers full access to visitors with specific needs.

Outdoor tables at Cala Gran bar

⑧ Café Parisien, Artà
MAP G3 ▪ C/Ciutat, 18 ▪ 971 835440

An artistic café *(see p79)* with a vintage air and a beautiful garden terrace, Café Parisien is an institution in Artà. It serves great snacks and modern seasonal cuisine.

⑨ The Beach Bar, S'Illot
MAP G4 ▪ Ronda del Mati, 9 ▪ 655 022250

This colourful bar serves up delicious fresh fruit mojitos, daiquiris and reasonably priced food on its beach-front terrace. More relaxed by day, it gets livelier on summer evenings.

⑩ Carpe Diem, Portopetro
MAP F6 ▪ Passeig des Port, 52 ▪ 608 348772

Live music and a breezy terrace make this bar a great place to spend the hot summer nights. Drop in for coffee and cakes during the day.

Places to Eat

PRICE CATEGORIES

For a three-course meal for one with half a bottle of wine (or equivalent meal), taxes and extra charges.

€ under €30 ■ €€ €30–50 ■ €€€ over €50

① S'Assecador, Porto Cristo
MAP G4 ■ C/Mar, 11 ■ 971 820826 ■ Closed Thu ■ €€

Enjoy a view of the marina while you tuck into a traditional Mallorcan meal at this restaurant decorated with Moroccan tilework.

② Punto 3, Manacor
MAP G4 ■ Hotel Son Amoixa Vell, Ctra Cales de Mallorca, km 3.4 ■ 971 846292 ■ Closed Tue ■ €€€

A romantic restaurant with a beautiful terrace, Punto 3 offers an à la carte menu featuring seasonal as well as daily recommendations.

③ Sa Cuina, Portocolom
MAP G5 ■ Ctra S'Horta-Portocolom; C/Vapor de Santueri, s/n ■ 971 824080 ■ Closed Thu & Jan ■ €

The food here combines traditional Mallorcan dishes and modern international cuisine. The decor is a nice mix of traditional and contemporary.

④ Celler Sa Sinia, Portocolom
MAP G5 ■ C/Pescadors, 28 ■ 971 824323 ■ Closed Sun ■ €€€

Chef Biel Perelló is a local legend: his delicious seafood-based menu has made Sa Sinia one of the best restaurants on the island. Try the lobster stew.

⑤ Ca'n Martina, Portopetro
MAP F6 ■ Paseo del Puerto, 56 ■ 971 657517 ■ €€

Come for freshly caught seafood and expertly cooked Mallorcan specialities, including black paella. The menu also includes standard children's food, such as burgers.

⑥ Es Cantonet, Santanyí
MAP F6 ■ Plaça Bernareggi, 2 ■ 971 163407 ■ Closed Sun ■ €€

Creative Mediterranean fare served in a historic Mallorcan building.

⑦ L'Arcada, Cala Figuera
MAP F6 ■ Calle Virgen del Carmen, 80 ■ 971 645032 ■ €€

With the most central spot on the port and the best views, L'Arcada serves fresh fish dishes depending on the day's catch.

⑧ La Costa, Portocolom
MAP G5 ■ C/Sivines, 5 ■ 676 366757 ■ Closed Nov–May ■ €€

Tasty Mediterranean dishes and fresh seafood feature on the menu of this romantic clifftop restaurant.

⑨ Port Blau, Colònia de Sant Jordi
MAP E6 ■ C/Gabriel Roca, 67 ■ 971 656555 ■ Closed Tue, Jan & Dec ■ €

Uses fish caught around Illa de Cabrera, served up in vast portions in an open dining area on the port.

⑩ Tomeu Caldentey Cuiner, Sa Coma
MAP G4 ■ C/Liles ■ 971 569663 ■ €€€

A Michelin-starred restaurant with a modern design, which offers three creative fixed-price tasting menus.

Chef's table at Es Molí d'en Bou

See map on p118

📕10 Central Plain

A visit to Mallorca is only really complete after an exploration of the vast and mostly flat Es Pla (The Plain). People often argue about whether the mountains or coast better represents the real Mallorca, but the true heart of the island is surely to be found in the villages of this central region, which still to this day make few concessions to tourism. This is the island's workshop – where food is grown and where most of the leather-workers, potters and the manufacturers of traditional *robes de llengües* (tongues of flame) textiles and the prized artificial pearls are based.

Old windmill near Montuïri

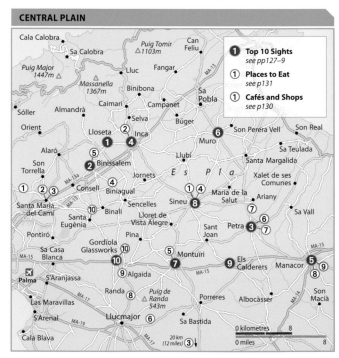

CENTRAL PLAIN

1 Top 10 Sights
see pp127–9

1 Places to Eat
see p131

1 Cafés and Shops
see p130

Almond trees in blossom, Lloseta

1 Lloseta
MAP D3

Traditionally part of the leather-crafting enterprises in the area, this town is situated on a sloping foothill. It has a tree-lined approach, a pretty little central square and several good restaurants.

2 Binissalem
MAP D3

Do not be put off by its rather workaday appearance from the highway. Hidden behind commercial enterprises, the historic centre (see p130) dates back to the ancient Romans, and is now dominated by centuries-old stone mansions that are very much worth a stroll around. The town's wealth arose from its preeminence as the island's wine producer, starting in the early 1500s. In recent years, after a century or so of decline, its reputation has again been on the rise, as evidenced by the important vineyard outlets along the main road.

3 Petra
MAP F4

This small town is the place of birth of Junípero Serra. At 36 years of age, the pioneering Franciscan monk travelled to America and Mexico and, after many arduous journeys on foot, founded missions in both Los Angeles and San Francisco. The houses lining the narrow alleys have changed little since Serra's time here. The town makes the most of its famous son, and all places associated with Serra are well marked. These include a humble building in Carrer Barracar Alt where he was born. Next to this is a small museum. Opened in 1955 and devoted to his life and work, it includes wooden models of the nine American missions established by Serra, though there is no reference to the Native Americans who had the rather dubious privilege of being evangelized. At the end of the street where the Serra family house stands is the 17th-century monastery of Sant Bernat. Majolica panels down a side street next to the monastery pay tribute to the monk.

Juniper Serra memorial, Petra

4 Inca
MAP E3

One of the many stops on the train journey from Palma to Sa Pobla, Inca, is a modern industrial place, but visitors come for the cheap leather goods found in Avinguda General Luque and Gran Via de Colon. Thursday, market day, is Inca's busiest time, trading in souvenirs, household goods, flowers and food. The town is also known for its traditional cuisine, including *caracoles* (snails), and its wine cellars turned into restaurants.

Leather handbags, Inca market

Figure of Christ at the Església de Nostra Senyora dels Dolors, Manacor

MALLORCA'S WINDMILLS

Mallorca is famous for its hundreds of windmills, especially in the region of Es Pla. These ingenious devices have been used in the Mediterranean since at least the 7th century. Now replaced by motorized pumps, most of the stone windmills have fallen into disrepair. However, in the region between Palma, Algaida and Llucmajor, ecology-minded farmers have repaired and renovated their old windmills.

The adjacent belfry has wonderful views of the area *(see p48)*. The town's Museu Etnológic is also worth a visit, and houses furniture, tools, costumes and instruments.

5 Manacor
MAP F4

Mallorca's second city is famous for being the home town of former world No. 1 tennis champion Rafael Nadal and for artificial pearl factories, of which Perlas Majorica *(see p130)* is the best known. The method of pearl production can be witnessed on the free tour. Also worth a look inside is the Església de Nostra Senyora dels Dolors, where pilgrims line up to kiss the feet of a figure of Christ.

6 Muro
MAP E3

This is a pleasant, sleepy town full of old mansions and dominated by the church of Sant Joan Baptista.

Nostra Senyora dels Àngels church, Sineu

7 Montuïri
MAP E4

Built on a hill, the town of Montuïri is famous for its agricultural produce. Nineteen of the original twenty-four windmills still stand as testimony to the town's former glory, striking in the landscape. The Ermita de Sant Miquel *(see p45)* is nearby, offering good views and a café-restaurant.

8 Sineu
MAP E3

At the geographical centre of the island, this hilly little town is distinguished by its impressive church, Nostra Senyora dels Àngels *(see p47)*, a medieval structure with a bell tower that soars above a huddle of old stone cottages. Nearby is the main square, Sa Plaça, the site of a large farmers' market every Wednesday morning.

9 Els Calderers

MAP E4 ■ Follow signs from MA-15 ■ 971 526069 ■ Open Apr–Oct: 10am–6pm daily; Nov–Mar: 10am–5pm daily ■ Adm ■ www.elscalderers.com

This country house chronicles 200 years of local gentry life in a modest version of La Granja (see pp20–21). Displays of traditional methods are part of the tour, and you can see historic breeds of Mallorcan farm animals.

Dining room, Els Calderers

10 Gordiola Glassworks

MAP D4 ■ Ctra Palma-Manacor, km 19, Algaida ■ 971 665046 ■ Open 9am–6pm Mon–Sat, 9am–1:30pm Sun ■ www.gordiola.com

The glassworks were founded in 1719, but the present castle-like, Neo-Gothic building dates from the 1960s. The fascinating place offers visitors a unique opportunity to watch glass-blowers at work, and its world-class museum of glass also fires enthusiasm for the craft. An on-site shop sells everything from inexpensive trinkets to chandeliers fit for a castle.

A DAY'S DRIVE THROUGH ES PLA

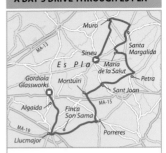

▶ MORNING

Begin in the north of Es Pla, at the medieval town of **Sineu** and be sure to visit the church of **Nostra Senyora dels Àngels** (see p47). Stroll around and stop for a drink and a snack at **Café Sa Plaça** (see p130). Proceed north to **Muro** for a look at the handsome Sant Joan Baptista church and the fascinating Museu Etnològic.

Drive on through pretty Santa Margalida, then Maria de la Salut.

By now, it should be lunchtime, so continue on to **Petra** (see p127) to have a wonderfully elegant meal at **Sa Plaça** (see p131), and to check out the hometown of the famous missionary Franciscan monk Junípero Serra (see p89).

AFTERNOON

After lunch, make the way on through Sant Joan and then to appealing **Montuïri**, with its signature windmills. Next, cut down to Porreres and take the road from there to Llucmajor. Be sure to stop off along the way for a walk around the quaintly picturesque grounds and gardens of the Finca Son Sama mansion.

The last leg of the journey is to head back north to **Algaida** (see p54), being sure to pop into Raïms for a look at its timeless charm.

Finally, just to the west of Algaida, take a prolonged tour of the **Gordiola Glassworks**, with its superb museum and shop.

See map on p126

Cafés and Shops

1 Café Sa Plaça, Sineu

MAP E3 ▪ Sa Plaça, 17 ▪ 971 520664

A pleasant café *(see p79)* in main square, by the church of Santa María.

2 ReCamper, Inca

MAP E3 ▪ Poligono Industrial, off main road ▪ 971 888233

The famous Spanish brand's shoes are made right here and visitors can have first pick of the newest styles at reduced prices. Follow the billboards featuring a huge foot.

Browsing the ReCamper outlet

3 Artesanía Textíl Bujosa, Santa Maria del Camí

MAP D3 ▪ C/Bernardo Santa Eugenia, 53 (E of Bunyola) ▪ 971 620054

The only manufacturer of *robes de llengües* (tongues of flame cloth) that still uses traditional methods on antique looms *(see p85)*. Tablecloths and other furnishings are sold.

4 Bodega Biniagual, Binissalem

MAP D3 ▪ Camí de Muro, 11 ▪ 971 511 524, 689 183954 ▪ www.bodega biniagual.com

The tiny village of Biniagual was restored from ruins, and now once again produces wine. This bodega has become one of the most prestigious wineries here *(see p82)*. Tours and tastings need to be booked in advance.

5 José L Ferrer, Binissalem

MAP D3 ▪ C/Conquistador, 103 ▪ 971 100100 ▪ Open Mar–Oct: 10am–7pm Mon–Sat (Nov–Feb: until 2pm Sat), 10am–3pm Sun; book ahead for wine tastings ▪ www.vinosferrer.com

This famous winery is worth a stop for the tour and the wine-tasting. Their reds are made from Mantonegro and Callet grapes, and the white from Moll.

6 Bar Ca'n Tomeu, Petra

MAP F4 ▪ C/Sol, 47 ▪ 971 561023

By the main square, this bar has a local feel and decor. The menu features *pa amb oli (see p76)*, tapas, salads and other more elaborate dishes.

7 Miquel Oliver, Petra

MAP F4 ▪ C/Font, 26 ▪ 971 561117 ▪ www.miqueloliver.com

Found in the little town of Petra, this bodega has a reputation for great dry white wines. Among many vintages, the Muscat Original is generally regarded as the best pick. Tours must be booked in advance.

8 Perlas Majorica, Manacor

MAP F4 ▪ Vía Palma, 9 ▪ 971 550900

This is the island's best-known imitation pearl factory, where the gems are made and then skilfully set into necklaces and bracelets by craftsmen. Tour the factory and browse the finished pieces in the shop.

9 Art-Metall, Manacor

MAP F4 ▪ Menendez Pelayo, 38 ▪ 971 559827

The place to find the wrought-iron objects seen all over the island, such as candelabras and mirrors.

10 Gordiola Glassworks, Baixos

A great collection *(see p129)*, of glass from around the world from ancient to modern, and an amazing array of glass merchandise.

See map on p126

Places to Eat

PRICE CATEGORIES

For a three-course meal for one with half a bottle of wine (or equivalent meal), taxes and extra charges.
....

€ under €30 ■ €€ €30–50 ■ €€€ over €50

① Molí des Torrent, Santa Maria del Camí

MAP D3 ■ Ctra de Bunyola, 75 ■ 971 140503 ■ Closed Wed, Thu ■ €€

Set in a restored windmill, Molí des Torrent serves traditional Mallorcan dishes with a German twist. There is also an excellent wine list.

② Celler Sa Sini, Santa Maria del Camí

MAP D3 ■ Plaça Hostals, 20 ■ 971 620252 ■ Closed Mon ■ €

Cozy and delightfully old-fashioned, this traditional Mallorcan restaurant dishes up local favourites, such as *frit mallorquí (see p76)*, and good pizzas.

③ Es Cantonet, Santanyí

MAP F6 ■ Plaça Bernareggi, 2 ■ 971 163407 ■ €

Located in an ancient townhouse, this traditional Mallorcan restaurant offers delicious main courses that are prepared using local ingredients. The menu changes seasonally.

④ Celler Es Grop, Sineu

MAP E3 ■ C/Major, 18 ■ 971 520187 ■ Closed Mon ■ €

The restaurant is housed in an atmospheric wine bodega. Choose from *lechona* (suckling pig), *arroz brut* (rice soup), *tumbet* (stewed vegetables) and *caracoles* (snails).

⑤ Restaurant Xorri, Montuïri

MAP E4 ■ C/Mayor, 2 ■ 971 644133 ■ €

A classic country eatery, this is a good place to sit out on the terrace with some great local food and a glass of wine and soak up the view.

⑥ Es Mirador, Llucmajor

MAP D5 ■ Finca Son Sama, Ctra Llucmajor-Porreres, km 3.5 ■ 971 120 959 ■ Closed Sun & mid-Dec–Feb ■ €€

Enjoy à la carte traditional fare, or sample the tasting menu as you take in the terrific views from the terrace.

⑦ Sa Plaça, Petra

MAP F4 ■ Plaça Ramon Llull, 4 ■ 971 561646 ■ Closed Tue ■ €€

Enjoy excellent traditional as well as modern fare at this charming, family-run restaurant with a small patio.

⑧ Es Recó de Randa, Algaida

MAP D4 ■ C/Font, 21, Randa ■ 971 660997 ■ €€

A tranquil place with inventive cuisine, which includes aubergine (eggplant) stuffed with salt cod.

⑨ Ca'n Mateu, Algaida

MAP D4 ■ Ctra Vieja de Manacor, km 21 ■ Closed Tue, D ■ 971 665036 ■ €€

Set in a 400-year-old inn and popular with locals, this spot serves traditional dishes, such as snails in broth.

⑩ Sa Torre de Santa Eugenia, Santa Eugenia

MAP D3 ■ Ctra de Santa Maria a Sencelles ■ 971 144011 ■ Closed L Tue–Fri, D Sat & Sun ■ €€

This restaurant in the 15th-century cellar of an ancient family house serves delicious Mediterranean food.

Tables at Sa Torre de Santa Eugenia

Streetsmart

**Historic train travelling between
Palma and Sóller**

Getting To and Around Mallorca

Arriving by Air

Scheduled and charter flights connect Mallorca's **Palma Airport** with major Spanish and European cities. Visitors from USA will have to make the connection somewhere in Europe, usually in Madrid.

The airport is 11 km (6 miles) southeast of the capital, with taxis and buses taking visitors to the city and resorts. The **Aena** website displays all bus routes to destinations around the island. The number 1 bus operates regularly between the airport and the transport system in central Palma.

Air Nostrum (part of Iberia) and other carriers operate flights to Palma from Ibiza and Menorca.

Vueling, **Ryanair**, **Air Europa** and **Iberia** all offer flights between mainland Spain and Mallorca.

Arriving by Ferry

The **Trasmediterránea** ferry company operates from Barcelona, Valencia and Alicante to Palma, and **Baleària** sails to Alcúdia from Barcelona and from Dénia to Palma via Ibiza. Journeys take approximately 4–8 hours.

There are also regular ferries between Mallorca and the other Balearic islands. Baleària connects Alcúdia to Ciutadella in Menorca, and Palma to Ibiza. Trasmediterránea also runs a ferry service from Ibiza and Menorca to Palma. Some routes offer a choice of high-speed and standard ferries: check in advance.

Travelling by Train and Tram

There are three regular railway lines on the island run by CTM, all of which depart from Palma's Plaça d'Espanya: T1 runs to Inca, T2 to Sa Pobla and T3 (following much of the same route as T2) runs to Manacor. Buy tickets at the machines before boarding.

The privately owned **Tren de Sóller** has been operating for more than a century and offers special trips, for an extra cost, between April and October. A tram runs from Sóller to Port de Sóller *(see p73)*.

Travelling by Bus and Metro

Mallorca has an extensive bus network operated by **Consorci Transport Mallorca (CTM)**. The central station is at Plaça d'Espanya in Palma. Timetables and maps are available from the information office at the Plaça Espanya and they are also posted on the CTM website.

If you are making regular use of the public transport, buy a T-20 or T-40 pass at Plaça d'Espanya station; these offer 20 or 40 journeys (valid for a year). Be sure to validate the pass in the machine behind the driver. If paying in cash on the bus, be aware that only bank notes up to €20 are accepted. In the case of tickets that cost more than €20, you may pay up to €50 in cash.

CTM also operates the two metro lines that depart from Plaça d'Espanya; one for the city's university, and another for Marratxi. Tickets are available at the machines at the station. You can purchase them before boarding.

Travelling by Car and Motorbike

Driving is the only way to see some of the best sights *(see pp68–9)*. The Palma–Llucmajor, Palma–Sa Pobla and Palma–Manacor roads are the major highways. Other roads, though narrow and twisting, are mostly in good repair.

Cheap car rental can be found online. Most big agencies, including **Hertz** and **Europcar**, are represented at Palma Airport. Drivers must be 21 or over, with a driver's licence and a credit card. All European and US driving licences are valid in Spain for tourists; visitors from North America are not required to have an International Driving Permit (IDP), but it is recommended. Car seats for kids (compulsory for children under 135cm) cost extra. Note that you are not allowed to take hired cars from one island to another or from Mallorca to the mainland.

Filling stations are common along main roads but thin on the ground when you are off the beaten track. Be aware that some petrol stations may close on Sundays. Many will have self-serve 24-hour pumps that require a chip-and-PIN credit card.

Rush hour only affects Palma, but there may be tailbacks to and from the main beaches in the peak summer season.

Travelling by Taxi

Taxis in Mallorca are white. **Palma Taxis** have a red stripe; in other municipalities they have a different-coloured stripe. Fares are moderate and there are plenty of taxis in circulation in Palma and in the main resorts. Supplements are charged for baggage and for fares to and from the airport and the ports.

Travelling by Bicycle

Mallorca is a very popular destination for biking, with a mix of country lanes and mountain roads that appeal to cyclists. The road to Sa Calobra is a particular highlight for serious bike enthusiasts, but there are numerous excellent routes to try all over the island.

Experienced cyclists (as well as those with no experience) can rent equipment at **Pro Cycle Hire** in Pollença. There are several suppliers in Palma and the main resorts, including **Nano Bicycles**, which also runs tours, and **Palma on Bike**.

In Palma, public bicycles are offered free of charge for transit users over 18 years of age with valid T20 or T40 tickets (Mou-te Bé scheme). For more details, check the CTM website.

Travelling on Foot

Mallorca offers superb hiking routes, most notably the long-distance GR-221 (see p68). There are several mountain refuges (see p141) offering accommodation along the route; book them through the **Mallorcan Government** website.

The GR-222, another long-distance route that will eventually link Artà in the east with Lluc further west, is currently under-way: some short sections, most around the northeast coast, are already open. Numerous shorter trails, many of which are ideal for families with young children, can be found in natural parks, such as the S'Albufera wetlands or the Parc Natural de Mondragó (see pp58–9).

The Catalina Homar route is a wonderful 11-km- (6-mile-) long hike around Valldemossa. The start of the route is suitable for beginners, but only experienced hikers should carry on.

The government website has an excellent section dedicated to hikes across the island, with route maps available to download. It also has plenty of information on the GR-221. **Info Mallorca**, the official tourist website, also has information to download on the GR-221 and on family-friendly routes around the island.

DIRECTORY

ARRIVING BY AIR

Aena
w aena.es

Air Europa
w aireuropa.com

Air Nostrum
w airnostrum.es

Iberia
w iberia.com

Palma Airport
c 971 78 90 85

Ryanair
w ryanair.com

Vueling
w vueling.com

ARRIVING BY FERRY

Baleària
w balearia.com

Trasmediterránea
w trasmediterranea.es

TRAVELLING BY TRAIN AND TRAM

Tren de Sóller
w trendesoller.com

TRAVELLING BY BUS AND METRO

Consorci Transport Mallorca (CTM)
w tib.org

TRAVELLING BY CAR AND MOTORBIKE

Europcar
w europcar.co.uk

Hertz
w hertz.co.uk

TRAVELLING BY TAXI

Palma Taxis
c 971 201212
w radiotaxiciutat.com

TRAVELLING BY BICYCLE

Nano Bicycles
w nanobicycles.com

Palma on Bike
w palmaonbike.com

Pro Cycle Hire
w procyclehire.com

TRAVELLING ON FOOT

Info Mallorca
w infomallorca.net

Mallorcan Government
w conselldemallorca.net

Practical Information

Passports and Visas

EU citizens can enter Spain with just their valid ID card or passport. Citizens of the US, Australia, Canada and New Zealand need only a passport for automatic permission to stay for up to 90 days. Other nationalities should check with the Spanish consulate in their country and consult the **Spanish Ministry of Foreign Affairs** website.

Mallorca has the consulates of **Ireland**, the **UK** and the **US**.

Customs and Immigration

Passengers can import the following from EU countries: 800 cigarettes, 400 cigarillos, 200 cigars, 1 kg smoking tobacco, 10 litres of spirits over 22 per cent proof, 20 litres of alcoholic beverages under 22 per cent proof, 90 litres of wine (no more than 60 litres of sparking wine) and 110 litres of beer. Visitors from a non-EU country may bring in 200 cigarettes, one litre of spirits, four litres of wine, and 250 ml of perfume.

More information can be found on the website for the Spanish Ministry of Foreign Affairs and the **Spanish Tax Office**.

Travel Safety Advice

Visitors can get up-to-date travel safety information from the **UK Foreign & Commonwealth Office**, the **US Department of State** and the **Australian Department of Foreign Affairs and Trade**.

Travel Insurance

It is advisable to take out an insurance policy that covers cancellation or curtailment of your trip, theft or loss of money and baggage, and healthcare. EU citizens can receive basic free medical care with a European health insurance card, which must be obtained before travelling (note that dental care is not covered by EU health agreements, but is affordable in comparison to other EU countries or to USA).

It is a good idea to take out private medical insurance, even if your country has reciprocal medical arrangements with Spain. Then, should you require treatment while on holiday, you can simply pay for the care, keep the receipts and be reimbursed according to the terms of your policy.

Health

No vaccinations are required for Spain. You're advised to bring all medications that you need with you (Spanish pharmaceuticals may be different from those in your home country in name, dosage and form). Sunburn and heatstroke are the main sources of discomfort – wear a hat, use sunscreen and drink bottled water.

If you are seriously ill and need a doctor who speaks your language, ask your local consulate, hotel, pharmacy or tourist office for contacts, or check on **TripMedic** (endorsed by the European Comission). If you need someone who works under the EU health plan, make sure that the doctor works for the Spanish healthcare system; otherwise, be prepared to pay on the spot and be reimbursed later by your insurance company. Palma has two main public hospitals: **Hospital de Sant Joan de Déu** and **Hospital Universitario Son Espases**.

Pharmacists are well trained and a good source of advice for minor complaints. In Palma, many pharmacies (farmacias) will remain open 24 hours a day, including the **Farmacia Balanguera** in the city centre and the **Farmacia Ldo Ramón Alcover** in the Porto Pi area. All pharmacies are required to post a list of the pharmacies on duty (farmàcies de guàrdia) when closed, or you can find the nearest one to you by consulting the **COFIB** website.

Personal Security

Mallorca is generally very safe. However, petty crime, in particular pickpocketing, is rife. Often working in pairs, pickpockets create distractions – sometimes very elaborate ploys – then fleece the unwary. Be sure to leave all valuables, including your passport, behind in a hotel safety-deposit box – most rooms have them. Take as little cash as possible and keep mobile phones and other expensive items out of sight. Carry wallets in front pockets and ensure bags are strapped across your front. On the beach and in cafés and restaurants, always keep your belongings on your lap or about your person. Be cautious of any odd or unnecessary human contact: thieves often work in twos, so while one is catching your attention, the other is swiping your wallet.

More serious incidences of violence are rare. But, thieves occasionally carry knives – if you are threatened, hand over your belongings. If you need to report a crime, go to the nearest police station (comissaria) or visit the **Central Police Station**. Remember that you will need to have a copy of the crime report to claim anything on your insurance.

You may see members of three Spanish police forces on Mallorca. The **Policía Local** (local police) deal with petty theft and are the most visible, while the **Guardia Civil** are in charge of transport. It is unlikely that you will encounter the **Policía Nacional**, who will only attend to a more serious accident or crime.

Women travellers do not generally experience anything more than perhaps a catcall, and even that is becoming less common. Spain, which has a shocking record of domestic abuse, has been campaigning hard for gender equality, and there is growing awareness of what constitutes unacceptable and sexist behaviour.

Emergency Services

Dial the free **emergency number** in any type of emergency; they speak English and will alert the appropriate service.

There are also emergency **Fire Brigade** and **Coast Guard** services.

Languages

The local language is Mallorquí, a dialect of Catalan, but Castilian (Spanish) is also spoken everywhere. Signs are usually, but not always, in Catalan. Any efforts to speak Mallorquí, even a simple *bon dia* (good day) is usually warmly received. Many tourist workers also speak German, English and other languages.

DIRECTORY

PASSPORTS AND VISAS

Ireland
MAP S1 ◾ C/Sant Miquel, 68A–7º/8º, Palma
🌐 irlanda.es

Spanish Ministry of Foreign Affairs
🌐 exteriores.gob.es

UK
MAP P1 ◾ C/Convent dels Caputxins, 4 Edificio Orisba B 4ºD
🌐 gov.uk/government/world/organisations/british-consulate-palma-de-mallorca

US
MAP R2 ◾ C/Porto Pí, 8, 9ºD, Palma
📞 971 403707
🌐 es.usembassy.gov

CUSTOMS AND IMMIGRATION

Spanish Tax Office
🌐 agenciatributaria.es

TRAVEL SAFETY ADVICE

Australian Department of Foreign Affairs and Trade
🌐 dfat.gov.au

UK Foreign & Commonwealth Office
🌐 gov.uk/foreign-travel-advice

US Department of State
🌐 travel.state.gov

HEALTH

COFIB
🌐 cofib.es

Farmacia Balanguera
MAP R1 ◾ C/Balanguera, 15
📞 971 458788

Farmacia Ldo Ramón Alcover
MAP R2 ◾ Avda. de Joan Miró, 186
📞 971 909015

Hospital de Sant Joan de Déu
MAP S2 ◾ C. Sant Joan de Déu, 7
🌐 hsjdpalma.es

Hospital Universitario Son Espases
MAP S1 ◾ Carr. de Valldemossa, 79
🌐 hospitalsonespases.es

Trip Medic
🌐 tripmedic.com

PERSONAL SECURITY

Central Police Station (Comissaria)
MAP R1 ◾ C/Son Dameto 1, Palma
📞 971 225500

Guardia Civil
📞 971 774100

Policía Local
📞 092 (emergency)
📞 971 225500

Policía Nacional
📞 971 225200

EMERGENCY SERVICES

Coast Guard
📞 971 713151

Fire Brigade
📞 085

Emergency Number
📞 112

Travellers with Specific Needs

Mallorca is not especially equipped for visitors with specific needs, although things are improving considerably. The uneven streets of Palma's historic quarter are difficult to negotiate with a wheelchair, and some sights, due to their age and history, remain wholly or partially off limits to those with limited mobility. However, most newer attractions, hotels and restaurants are wheelchair-accessible, as is all public transport.

Several tour operators offer accessible holidays in Mallorca, and they can offer advice for planning an accessible trip. These include **Accessible Spain Travel**, **Can Be Done**, and **Travel Counsellors**.

The official tourist website, **Info.Mallorca**, has been designed to suit those with impaired sight and hearing: visit the "Accessibility" section for more information.

Currency and Banking

The official currency of Spain is the euro. It is subdivided into 100 cents (céntimos). Bank notes have the following denominations: 5, 10, 20, 50, 100, 200 and 500 (but very few places accept larger notes as they are difficult to break). Euro coins come in eight denominations: €1, €2, and 1, 2, 5, 10, 20 and 50 cents. Visitors from outside the eurozone should check the exchange rates at the time of travel.

ATMs are readily available and reliable throughout the island.

Spanish banks charge transaction fees, and your own bank may charge a fee for using a non-branch machines. All major credit cards are accepted in the larger hotels, restaurants and museums, but are often not accepted in smaller establishments.

Telephone and Internet

The country code for Spain is +34. A 3G or 4G broadband mobile will work, but check with your provider regarding any additional costs. Consider picking up a Spanish SIM card or a pay-as-you-go mobile (both widely available) if you are travelling from outside the EU. One can find these at outlets in larger resorts, including the department store at **El Corte Inglés** (see p85).

Many cafés, hotels and restaurants offer free Wi-Fi to guests, as do international eateries and coffee houses.

Postal Services

The Spanish postal service is quite reliable, although you should send important documents by certified (certificat) post. Letters take about 3 to 5 days to arrive in other EU countries, and from 5 to 7 days to arrive in North America. There are post offices in all the larger towns and resorts. Yellow letterboxes, usually with the word "correos" on them, are found across the island. Often, you can also drop off letters or postcards at the reception desk of your hotel. The **Main Post Office** in Palma is centrally located, near the cathedral.

TV, Radio and Newspapers

The state-owned RTVE (Radio Television España) operates five main channels: La 1 and La 2 have the standard TV schedule; 24 Horas broadcasts news around the clock; Clan is dedicated to kids' TV, and Teledeporte to sports. Most hotels subscribe to all the major international digital channels. In larger towns and resorts, plenty of bars offer big-screen TVs that show live sporting events, especially football.

Several local radio stations broadcast in English, such as Radio One Mallorca (93.8 FM), Talk Radio Europe (104.8 FM) and Spectrum (89.8 FM).

The main Spanish daily newspapers are *El País* (left-leaning) and *El Mundo* (right-leaning). Mallorca's most popular daily newspapers are *Ultima Hora* and *Diario de Mallorca*. Foreign language papers and magazines are readily available at news kiosks across the island.

Opening Hours

Shops in Mallorca are usually open Monday to Saturday from 9:30am until 8 or 9pm, and close for lunch around 1:30 or 2pm to 4:30 or 5pm. In the larger towns and resorts, big chains and department stores open from 10am to 9pm and do not close for lunch. They are often open on Sundays. Shops in the larger resorts may open only at weekends or even close during the winter.

Offices may be closed completely during the month of August, or they may only be open in the mornings. Banks are open 9:30am to 2pm, and some additionally open on a Thursday afternoon from 4 to 7pm, though a few operate a reduced time-table in summer. Churches open 8am to 1pm and from 6 to 8pm; some are open on Sunday mornings but prefer not to admit tourists.

The main post offices are open from 9am to 9pm, but most smaller branches close at 2pm.

Time Difference

Mallorca is on Central European Time, which is 1 hour ahead of GMT and 6 hours ahead of Eastern Standard Time. Spanish summer time (when the whole country switches to daylight saving time) begins on the last Sunday in March and ends on the last Sunday in October. Note that daylight saving time will come to an end in March 2021.

Electrical Appliances

The power supply in Spain is 220–225 volts. Sockets accept two-round-pin-style plugs, so an adaptor is needed for most non-continental appliances and a transformer for appliances operating on 100–120 volts. Some hotels and apartments are equipped with hair-dryers and irons, but kettles are rarely found.

Smoking

Although forbidden on public transport and in hotels and restaurants, smoking is much more common in Spain than in other parts of Europe. The outdoor tables at bars and restaurants are often occupied by smokers.

Weather

Mallorca has mild, humid winters and hot, dry summers. Expect daytime temperatures in winter to be above 12° C (53° F), and in summer not to fall below 30° C (86° F).

Summer is high season in Mallorca. This means gorgeous sunshine, warm seas – and, unfortunately, crowds. If you are looking for nightlife, then it is the perfect time to visit.

The main holiday month in Spain is August; this is when schools are shut and many offices also close, so prices can skyrocket. Spring and autumn are usually the best times for hiking and cycling.

Spring is also the best time for nature-lovers to visit, as birds are on the move and trees and wild flowers blossom. Autumn is also very appealing: there is still plenty of sunshine, the water is at its warmest and prices are lower. But winter also has its own charms: there are fewer options in terms of accommodation and restaurants, but you will have the beaches and hiking trails to yourself.

Visitor Information

The Info.Mallorca website (see p139) is an excellent resource. It provides a host of useful information on everything from where to stay to what to do, and you can also download booklets in PDF format directly from the site. The **Mallorcan Government** (see p135) website and Palma's official tourism website, **Visit Palma**, are also excellent sources. In Palma, visit the main tourist office on Plaça d'Espanya for information on what to do and see.

Other good sources include **See Mallorca** and **ABC Mallorca**, all of which both provide a huge directory of places to stay, as well as local news and information about what's on.

DIRECTORY

TRAVELLERS WITH SPECIFIC NEEDS

Accessible Spain Travel
W accessiblespaintravel.com

Can Be Done
W canbedone.co.uk

Info.Mallorca
W infomallorca.net

Travel Counsellors
W travelcounsellors.co.uk

POSTAL SERVICES

Main Post Office
MAP L4 ▪ C/Constitució 5, Palma
W correos.es

TV, RADIO AND NEWSPAPERS

Diario de Mallorca
W diariodemallorca.es

El Mundo
W elmundo.es

El País
W elpais.com

Ultima Hora
W ultimahora.es

VISITOR INFORMATION

ABC Mallorca
W abc-mallorca.com

See Mallorca
W seemallorca.com

Visit Palma
Plaça de la Reina 2, Palma
W visitpalma.com

Trips and Tours

All manner of trips and tours are available in Mallorca, from bus tours of Palma to curated wine tasting and hot-air ballooning trips. Tourist offices offer information on the options available in each area.

The hop-on hop-off bus service run by **City Sightseeing** is a very popular and convenient way of seeing Palma. You can also explore the city on two wheels with **Nano Bicycles** (see p135), or head out of town on the vintage **Sóller train and tram** (see p73).

If you are looking for thrills on your holiday, numerous operators, including **Mallorcan Adventure Sports** and **Experience Mallorca** offer a range of outdoor and adventure activities such as horse-riding, canyoning, sea caving as well as kite-surfing.

Gourmet enthusiasts can learn to make delicious local dishes through **The Galley Club**, or take a tour of the best Mallorcan vineyards with **Mallorca Wine Tours**.

Shopping

Great buys in Mallorca include deli products, such as hams, cheeses, and olive oil, as well as the wonderful local wines. Visitors should check which consumable products can be brought back to their home country.

Home to Spain's most famous shoe company, **Camper** (see p130), the island is a good place to buy shoes. Along with branded shoes, *espadrilles* (traditional Spanish shoes with rope soles) are a good informal option. Mallorca also has all the main Spanish chains, along with plenty of charming one-off stores.

There are two main sales periods, one in early January and another beginning on 1 July. All prices include VAT (IVA in Spanish), which is currently 21 per cent on most goods. Tax refunds are available on purchases that cost over €90.19 and which are being taken outside the EU. Ask at participating stores for more information.

Dining

Mallorca's eateries run the gamut from beachfront tapas bars and family-run taverns to chic Michelin-starred gourmet restaurants.

There is a wider range of restaurants serving cuisines from other areas of the world here than in other parts of Spain, and you will find options from around Europe, as well as many Thai, Japanese and Peruvian places. Vegetarian restaurants have proliferated in recent years, and there is now a much wider choice for vegetarians and vegans almost everywhere. Regional dishes that are suitable for non-meat eaters include *tumbet* (a tomato-rich vegetable stew), *eggs al modo de Sóller*, *tortilla española* (Spanish omelette) and Mahón-style beans. Local cheeses are also great. Try the creamy, nutty *queso mallorquín* and the cured cheese from Maó.

Many restaurants offer a good-value set-price lunch menu from Monday to Friday (menú del día), a great way to try places that might otherwise be beyond your budget.

In the cheaper bars it is worth trying tapas or *raciónes* (small plates), as these are most likely to be freshly prepared (a *ración* is often a big enough portion for two).

Mallorcan restaurants usually open from 1:30 to 3:30pm for lunch, and from 8:30 to 11pm for dinner, with most locals eating later. If you want to dine earlier, tapas bars fill the gap nicely and start serving from around 6:30pm.

Except in the main resorts, restaurants will rarely offer specific menus for children, although tapas provide an ideal solution if you are looking for small portions. Very few restaurants have high chairs, so it is best to bring your own or ring ahead to check.

Cafés are an integral part of Mallorcan life, and usually serve light meals and snacks along with coffee or breakfast, and many hotels cater to international tastes with a full breakfast buffet.

Locals rarely tip: they might drop a couple of coins on a restaurant bill if the service was good, or round up the price of a cup of coffee. However, there are different expectations of tourists, and it should be remembered that a lot of work on the island is seasonal, with many Mallorcans struggling to find work during the winter. Staff at restaurants and bars will be very appreciative if you add a 5 or 10 per cent tip to the bill, if you were happy with the service.

Accommodation

Many visitors to Mallorca book a package holiday, with accommodation included. The resorts are filled with apartment buildings and big hotels, which generally offer great value. However, independent travellers will find something to suit all tastes and budgets in Mallorca, whether they are looking for chic minimalism and plenty of services right in the heart of Palma, a remote mountain retreat, or cosy chintz in the countryside.

Most accommodation on the island falls into the following categories: hotels (these are rated between one and five stars); *hostals*, which are simple guest houses that may often resemble hotels, and should not be confused with youth hostels; B&Bs; villas; holiday apartments; and finally, youth hostels. Some monasteries also offer cheap, but very simple rooms (although strict curfews sometimes apply) – the tourist information offices in Mallorca can often book these for you or provide more detailed information.

There are a number of simple hikers' refuges along the GR-221, the long-distance walking path that runs along the island's northwestern coast (see p70). The accommodation here is basic, but simple meals are usually available (check in advance) and bedding can be rented if required. These refuges are maintained by the **Consell de Mallorca**. Advance booking is highly recommended.

For those seeking quiet, out-of-the-way places, another alternative is a rural getaway in *fincas* and *casas rurales*. These are hotels that occupy former country mansions or farmhouses, usually located in the interiors of the island. They can provide a degree of authenticity that is not found elsewhere. Rooms at these getaways are mostly furnished with period furniture as well as antiques, which accentuate the character of the place.

Some *fincas* are very high-class, and cater to the wealthy. Others are in ordinary country houses and may be surrounded by holiday bungalows and apartments. Details can also be found on the internet.

Mallorca has very few proper campsites, and those that exist generally only offer accommodation in bungalows or chalets rather than providing pitches for tents.

Rates are highest during July and August, with the best prices available in the off season in the spring and autumn. Note, however, that many establishments on the island, particularly in the main resorts, close during winter. Numerous general booking websites, such as **Booking.com** or **TripAdvisor**, offer options for accommodation in Mallorca, but it is always worth checking for the best prices directly with the establishment as they may be able to offer you a better deal.

If you are looking for something a bit different, **The Other Mallorca** specialises in luxury hotels and self-catering cottages, mainly at the top end of the price spectrum. **Airbnb**, a popular online marketplace for private property rentals, also has a number of excellent properties across Mallorca. Many of these available properties are unique and are priced much more competitively than traditional options for accommodation.

DIRECTORY

TRIPS AND TOURS

City Sightseeing
w city-ss.es/en/palma-de-mallorca

Experience Mallorca
w experience-mallorca.com

The Galley Club
w thegalleyclub.com

Mallorca Adventure Sports
w mallorcaadventuresports.com

Mallorca Wine Tours
w mallorcawinetours.com

ACCOMMODATION

Airbnb
w airbnb.com

Booking.com
w booking.com

Consell de Mallorca
w conselldemallorca.cat

The Other Mallorca
w theothermallorca.com

TripAdvisor
w tripadvisor.com

Places to Stay

PRICE CATEGORIES

For a standard, double room per night (with breakfast if included), taxes and extra charges.

€ under €100   €€ €100–200   €€€ over €200

Historic Lodgings

Es Castell, Binibona

MAP E2 ▪ C/Binibona, s/n ▪ 971 875154 ▪ www.fincaescastell.com ▪ €€

This family-run hotel in an old stone *finca* (farmhouse) has mountains on one side and orchards on the other. There are just 12 rooms here, each with exquisite fittings and wood-beamed ceilings. Breakfast features home-grown ingredients. Limited amenities for guests with specific needs.

Hotel Can Cera, Palma

MAP N4 ▪ C/San Francisco, 8 ▪ 971 715012 ▪ www.cancerahotel.com ▪ €€

Housed in a 17th-century palace, Can Cera is one of the old city's most attractive spots, right in the heart of Palma by the Plaça de Santa Eulàlia. Of its 12 boutique rooms, seven are suites, and all are beautifully appointed with period furniture. The hotel also has two restaurants and a spa.

Hotel Juma, Pollença

MAP E1 ▪ Plaça Major, 9 ▪ 971 534155 ▪ www.hoteljuma.com ▪ €€

This Modernista hotel is full of antiques. Many rooms overlook the square below; some have four-poster beds. A rooftop solarium with Jacuzzi offers fine views. There are no accessible facilities.

Cap Rocat, Cala Blava

MAP C5 ▪ Ctra d'Enderrocat, s/n ▪ 971 747878 ▪ www.caprocat.com ▪ €€€

Located 20 minutes from Palma Airport, this former military fortress sits on a private peninsula, overlooking Palma Bay and its own private beach. There are 24 lavishly appointed rooms and suites. Every five-star service is offered, including fine dining and a spa. It has also made efforts to reduce its ecological footprint through many sustainable initiatives.

Castell Son Claret

MAP B4 ▪ Ctra Es Capdellà-Galilea, km 1.7 ▪ 971 138629 ▪ www.castellsonclaret.com ▪ €€€

A 15th-century castle, remodelled and rebuilt over centuries, is now home to this sumptuous rural retreat. Stunning views and complete tranquillity combine with spa treatment facilities, pools, gardens and a magnificent restaurant, Zaranda *(see p81)*, to create the ultimate luxury experience.

Convent de la Missío, Palma

MAP N2 ▪ C/de la Missío, 7 ▪ 971 227347 ▪ www.conventdelamissio.com ▪ €€€

A 17th-century monastery richly converted into a stylish boutique hotel. Minimalist furnishings in shades of white complement the historic setting. The building's old refectory is now an elegant restaurant. Limited facilities for guests with specific needs.

Hotel Llenaire, Port de Pollença

MAP E1 ▪ Camí de Llenaire, km 3.8 ▪ 971 535251 ▪ www.hotel-llenaire.com ▪ €€€

Elegant and charming, this Mallorcan manor house offers 11 guest rooms, an outdoor infinity pool and a sauna along with other modern amenities. Its beautiful location guarantees lovely views over the bay. Amenities for guests with specific needs are not available.

Palacio Ca Sa Galesa, Palma

MAP C4 ▪ C/Miramar, 8 ▪ 971 715400 ▪ www.palaciocasagalesa.com ▪ €€€

One of Mallorca's most lavish hotels is set in a 16th-century palace behind the cathedral. Sumptuous architectural features and antique decoration abound, including bathrooms with stained-glass windows. Some suites have Jacuzzis. Limited facilities for guests with specific needs.

San Lorenzo, Palma

MAP J3 ▪ C/Sant Llorenç, 14 ▪ 971 728200 ▪ www.hotelsanlorenzo.com ▪ €€€

This 17th-century manor house in Palma's central medieval quarter has been restored with care, preserving its Mallorcan character. Wrought iron details, beamed ceilings, and stone-and-tile accents create an elegant setting. Amenities include an outdoor pool and a bar. Some areas have facilities for guests with specific needs.

Design and Boutique Hotels

Cas Ferrer Nou Hotelet, Alcúdia
MAP F2 ▪ C/Pou Nou, 1 ▪ 971 897542 ▪ www.nouhotelet.com ▪ €€
Each of the six rooms and suites in this cosmopolitan hotel are beautifully and individually decorated in unique themes, inspired by parts of the Mediterranean. The roof terrace is ideal for relaxing. The hotel has limited access for those with specific needs.

Desbrull, Pollença
MAP E1 ▪ Marquès Desbrull, 7 ▪ 971 535055 ▪ www.desbrull.com ▪ Closed Dec–Jan ▪ €€
This attractive townhouse blends period and modern aesthetics. Its public spaces are decorated with art (some for sale) by local artists. The contemporary feel continues through to the six suites, which have sleek, modern bathrooms.

Son Cleda, Sineu
MAP E3 ▪ Plaça es Fossar, 7 ▪ 971 521027 ▪ www.hotelsoncleda.com ▪ €€
The comfortable rooms of this delightful townhouse are traditionally designed, but are equipped with modern amenities; some are wheelchair accessible as well. The pretty terrace in the restaurant-café is perfect for enjoying the sunshine and the views. The hotel offers bikes for rent as well as bike tours.

Finca Ca N'Ai, Sóller
MAP C2 ▪ Cami Son Sales, 50 ▪ 971 632494 ▪ www.canai.com ▪ €€€
Owned by a local family for 14 generations, this country estate has been converted into a delightful hotel. It boasts of large, luxurious suites, but there are limited facilities for guests with specific needs. Children under 16 are not allowed.

Hospes Maricel, Palma
MAP R2 ▪ Ctra D'Andratx, 11 (MA-1c) ▪ 971 707744 ▪ www.hospes.com ▪ €€€
This 17th-century palace is full of modern features, such as a large infinity pool, a spa and wellness centre and an excellent restaurant. All of the rooms have king-size beds and plasma TVs.

Hotel Calatrava, Palma
MAP P6 ▪ Plaça de Llorenç Villalonga, 8 ▪ 971 728 110 ▪ www.boutiquehotelcalatrava.com ▪ €€€
A boutique gem in the old quarter, this hotel boasts a fabulous roof terrace and a chic interior that pairs contemporary design with beamed ceilings and exposed stone walls. Many of the spacious suites enjoy wonderful views. Amenities include a spa area, which is available for private use.

Petit Palace Hotel Tres, Palma
MAP K4 ▪ C/Apuntadors, 3 ▪ 971 717333 ▪ www.hoteltres.com ▪ €€€
With its elegant fusion of modern design and 500-year-old architecture, Hotel Tres is perfect for those seeking both

comfort and a sense of history. Its position makes it convenient to visit the major sights of Palma.

Son Brull, Pollença
MAP E1 ▪ Ctra Palma-Pollença, km 50 ▪ 971 535353 ▪ www.sonbrull.com ▪ Closed Jan & Dec ▪ €€€
Rural style sits alongside avant-garde design here. Rooms and suites have modern facilities, and the spa and swimming pools offer relaxation. Two private villas offer two rooms and bathrooms each, as well as a private pool and garden area. The restaurant specializes in local cuisine; and organizes cookery classes too.

Mountain Retreats

Can Furiós Petit Hotel, Binibona
MAP E2 ▪ Camí Vell Binibona, 11 ▪ 971 515260 ▪ www.can-furios.com ▪ €€
Set in a 16th-century villa, this lovely mountain retreat is now a fabulous hotel with gardens, terraces, shaded patios and an inviting pool. Rooms are richly decorated – several have antique canopy beds – and the restaurant is excellent. Note that it is not wheelchair accessible.

Ca'n Reus, Fornalutx
MAP D2 ▪ C/l'Alba, 26, Fornalutx ▪ 971 639866 ▪ www.canreushotel.com ▪ €€
A rustic yet elegant hotel, filled with a mix of plain and period decor. There is a simple pool in the garden, and stunning valley and mountain views. Facilities unavailable for guests with specific needs.

Ca'n Verdera, Fornalutx
MAP D2 ▪ C/des Toros, 1 ▪ 971 638203 ▪ www. canverdera.com ▪ €€
Actress Sophia Loren has stayed in this chic and modern remodelling of a huge old house. The hotel has 11 uniquely designed suites and rooms. Limited amenities for guests with specific needs.

Costa d'Or, Deià
MAP C2 ▪ Lluc-Alcari ▪ 971 639025 ▪ Apr–Oct ▪ www.hoposa.es ▪ €€
A quaint cluster of rough-stone buildings set against verdant rocky promontories, this hotel provides simple yet comfortable accommodation. It has a lovely pine grove, a pool, a tennis court and a mini-golf course. Limited facilities for guests with specific needs. Children under 14 are not permitted.

Belmond La Residencia, Deià
MAP C2 ▪ Son Canals, s/n ▪ 971 639011 ▪ www. belmond.com ▪ €€€
The 18th- century manor house overlooks the Deià valley, rising high above the road and affording unparalleled views of the sea and mountains. This hotel is popular with a discerning clientele, who can expect to be pampered in perfect privacy. Some sections are wheelchair accessible.

Ca's Xorc, Sóller
MAP C2 ▪ Ctra Sóller-Deià, km 56.1 ▪ 971 638280 ▪ www.casxorc.com ▪ €€€
Located above the Sóller Valley, eye-to-eye with the Serra de Tramuntana, this country house has a pool, a restaurant and

breathtaking views. Original art and Moroccan-style touches create a sense of luxury. Limited accessible facilities for guests with specific needs.

Es Molí, Deià
MAP C2 ▪ Ctra Valldemossa-Deià ▪ 971 639000 ▪ www.esmoli. com ▪ €€€
Rooms at this hotel, which clings to the hill above the town, are traditional (those in the annexe are cheaper). There is also a pool, tennis court and private beach.

Gran Hotel Son Net, Puigpunyent
MAP B3 ▪ Castillo de Son Net ▪ 971 147000 ▪ www. sonnet.es ▪ €€€
Set in a mountain-ringed valley, this 17th-century palace is filled with antiques. The beautifully tended grounds feature a large pool, a gym and tennis courts. Each room has a unique character.

L'Hermitage Hotel & Spa, Orient
MAP D3 ▪ Ctra Alaró-Bunyola ▪ 971 180303 ▪ www.hermitage-hotel. com ▪ €€€
This is a rural haven of peace and tranquillity. A beautifully restored manor house, L'Hermitage was once a monastery and offers pretty gardens, breathtaking scenery and a first-class restaurant.

Mirabo, Valldemossa
MAP C3 ▪ Ctra Valldemossa km 16 ▪ 661 285215 ▪ www.mirabo.es ▪ €€€
The work of American modern architect Frank Lloyd Wright inspired the renovation of this country house. Only the number

of rooms and the infinity pool detract from the impression that it might be an artist's home.

Son Ametler, Moscari
MAP E2 ▪ C/Son Riera, s/n ▪ 678 989071 ▪ www. hotelsonametler.com ▪ Closed Nov–Feb ▪ €€€
Set in rural surroundings amid the foothills of the Serra de Tramuntana, this hotel offers eight guest rooms in a modernised old *finca*. There's an outdoor pool and a residents' restaurant serving outstanding food.

Resort Hotels

Sis Pins, Port de Pollença
MAP E1 ▪ Passeig d'Anglada Camarassa, 77 ▪ 971 867050 ▪ www. hotelsispins.com ▪ €
A traditional hotel close to the sea, once favoured by author Agatha Christie, offering elegant rooms and welcoming service.

Tres Playas, Colònia de Sant Jordi
MAP E6 ▪ C/Esmeralda ▪ 971 655151 ▪ €€
Here, terraces descend to the sea, punctuated with beautiful gardens and pools. Activities on offer include water polo, aqua classes and tennis. All the spacious rooms have sea views and balconies. There are also bars, restaurants and a beauty salon.

Hotel Es Port, Port de Sóller
MAP C2 ▪ C/Antonio Montis, 10 ▪ 971 631650 ▪ www.hotelesport.com ▪ €€€
A historic house and tower set in grounds with a spa, tennis courts, terraces,

pools and fountains. Some rooms are in the modern annexe, others are in the gardens, but the most atmospheric are in the old house. Facilities unavailable for guests with specific needs.

Hotel Formentor, Port de Pollença
MAP E1 ▪ Playa de Formentor, s/n ▪ 971 899100 ▪ www.barcelo. com ▪ €€€
It is the island's first and grandest resort (see p108). Guests include the who's who of the 20th century: the Dalai Lama, Chaplin, Churchill, the Windsors and Placido Domingo. A spectacular setting, a private beach, lovely gardens, and every luxury guests could wish for.

Jumeirah Port Sóller Hotel & Spa, Port de Sóller
MAP C2 ▪ C/Belgica, s/n ▪ 971 637888 ▪ www. jumeirah.com ▪ €€€
Often described as one of the finest hotels across the whole Mediterranean, this establishment offers unrivalled luxury. Sitting above the port, it boasts great views in every direction. The spa is also excellent.

La Reserva Rotana, Manacor
MAP F4 ▪ Camí de Bendris, km 3 ▪ 971 845685 ▪ www.reserva-rotana.com ▪ €€€
A meditative swing above the pool is reason enough to come here. The rooms are huge, the service is enthusiastic, and the grounds include a golf course and tennis court. Limited accessible facilities for guests with specific needs.

St Regis Mardavall Hotel, Costa d'en Blanes
MAP B4 ▪ Ctra Palma-Andratx, 19 ▪ 971 629629 ▪ www.marriott.com ▪ €€€
By the sea and with easy access to Palma, this haven of luxury offers relaxation and pampering. Excellent spa and Michelin-starred dining.

Villa Italia, Port d'Andratx
MAP A4 ▪ Camino de San Carlos, 13 ▪ 971 674 011 ▪ www.hotelvillaitalia. com ▪ €€€
A gracious Italianate structure dating from the 1920s, with luxury suites or annex rooms. The restaurant is fabulous. Note that the hotel has no facilities for those with specific needs.

Seaside Hotels

Hostal Playa, Colònia Sant Jordi
MAP E6 ▪ C/Major, 25 ▪ 971 655256 ▪ www. restauranteplaya.com ▪ €
Adorably old-fashioned and just a little bit funky, this secret hideaway has a wonderful patio-terrace on a practically private beach, composed of sand and large flat rocks. Old ceramics decorate every room, enhancing the whitewashed, red-tiled character of the place. The hotel has no facilities for those with specific needs.

Aimia Hotel, Port de Sóller
MAP C2 ▪ C/Santa Maria del Camí, 1 ▪ 971 631200 ▪ www.aimiahotel.com ▪ €€
Just a stone's throw from the seafront, this modern,

family-run hotel is perfect for a relaxing break, but activities are plentiful in the vicinity, too. Facilities include a pool, a spa, a restaurant and a bar.

Hotel Bahia, Port de Pollença
MAP E1 ▪ Passeig Voramar, 29 ▪ 971 866562 ▪ www.hoposa.es ▪ €€
An appealing 19th-century summer home with shutters and a seafront patio, surrounded by gardens and pines. The views are excellent, and the mood relaxed and friendly. Rooms are spacious, many with terraces, beamed ceilings and interesting antiques. Bike rental and storage is available; however, wheelchair access is limited.

Hotel Playa Mondragó, Portopetro
MAP F6 ▪ C/Mondragó, 12 ▪ 971 657752 ▪ www. playamondrago.com ▪ €€
Located within the Mondragó Nature Reserve, a short walk from the beach, this lively hotel has a warm ambience. Rooms have mini-fridges and coffee making facilities as well as private balconies. One-bedroom apartments are also available.

Miramar, Port de Pollença
MAP E1 ▪ Passeig Anglada Camarassa, 39 ▪ 971 866400 ▪ www. hotel-miramar.net ▪ €€
A stylish establishment with beamed ceilings, a terrace with a sea view, and lush gardens. Rooms are quiet and comfortable and its elegant patios are graced with antiques and ceramics. Amenities unavailable for guests with specific needs.

Hotel Cala Sant Vicenç

MAP E1 ▪ C/Maressers, 2 ▪ 971 530 250 ▪ www.hotelcala.com ▪ €€

This handsome hotel is surrounded by lush gardens. Classically elegant rooms offer every comfort and there are two superb restaurants as well as a snack bar by the pool.

H10 Punta Negra Hotel, Costa d'en Blanes

MAP B4 ▪ C/Punta Negra, 12 ▪ 971 680762 ▪ www.h10hotels.com ▪ €€€

Well-established hotel sited on its own peninsula, it is within easy reach of secluded coves. Every amenity is on hand.

Hotel Can Simoneta, Canyamel

MAP H3 ▪ Ctra Arta-Canyamel, km 8 ▪ 971 816110 ▪ www.cansimoneta.com ▪ €€€

Surrounded by fragrant gardens and perched on a clifftop overlooking coves and turquoise waters, this 150-year-old *finca* boasts rooms with four-poster beds, wooden beams and contemporary furnishings. Only those over 16 are permitted here.

Hotel Petit, Cala Fornells

MAP B4 ▪ Ctra de Cala Fornells, 78 ▪ 971 685405 ▪ www.petitcalafornells.com ▪ €€€

High over the bay, with panoramic views and several levels of terraces, this gem has all the amenities of a resort. The decor is a gorgeous blend of Spanish and Moroccan. There are four pools and a secluded beach. Limited wheelchair access available.

Agroturismo (Farmhouses)

Ca'n Moragues, Artá

MAP G3 ▪ C/Pou Nou, 12 ▪ 971 829509 ▪ www.canmoragues.com ▪ €€

A small and exclusive hotel set in a refurbished 18th-century manor house in the heart of Artà. Every comfort has been seen to in the unique combination of antique and modern furnishings. Limited facilities available for visitors with specific needs.

Ca's Curial, Sóller

MAP C2 ▪ C/La Villalonga, 23 ▪ 971 633332 ▪ www.cascurial.com ▪ €€

Guests get a lot of space and luxury for the price here. The hotel has a rustic feel, but is well-equipped, with every modern amenity available. It is set in a fragrant orange grove just a few minutes from central Sóller. The views of the jagged, pine-covered mountains; are stunning: enjoy them while sitting by the terrace pool. Wheelchair access is limited to some areas. Only guests over 16 are allowed here.

Fincahotel Can Estades, Calvià

MAP B4 ▪ Camí de Son Pillo, 15 ▪ 971 670558 ▪ www.can-estades.com ▪ €€

A 16th-century estate with lush gardens and great views. Rooms are spacious and have traditional furniture. Suites with kitchens are also available here. Children above 12 are welcome, as are pets (by request). There is limited wheelchair accessibility.

Raïms, Algaida

MAP D4 ▪ C/Ribera, 24 ▪ 971 665157 ▪ www.finca-raims.com ▪ €€

The self-catering apartments here are modern, but this country house has kept its old wine cellars and stone floors. Enjoy the sense of timelessness while lazing by the pool. Some areas are wheelchair accessible.

Sa Carrotja, Ses Salines

MAP E6 ▪ Sa Carrotja, 7 ▪ 971 649053 ▪ www.sacarrotja.com ▪ €€

This pretty 16th-century farmhouse has been modernized without losing its country charm. Guests can sample delicious local cuisine made from the proprietor's organic produce. Bicycles are also available for use. Though a quiet, refined choice, note that this is an adults-only hotel.

Ses Rotes Velles, Campos–Colònia Sant Jordi

MAP E6 ▪ Ctra Campos-Colonia Sant Jordi, km 8.7 ▪ 971 656159 ▪ Closed Dec–Feb ▪ sesrotesvelles.es ▪ €€

Immaculate lawns set off beautiful flower gardens, a vibrant counterpoint to the rich ochre of the bungalows. The food is some of the island's best.

Son Siurana, Alcúdia

MAP F2 ▪ Ctra Palma-Alcúdia, km 42.8 ▪ 971 549662 ▪ www.sonsiurana.com ▪ €€

Set in pretty woodland, this family-run agroturismo comprises a rural mansion (dating from 1784) and guesthouses. Despite its rusticity, it offers many modern amenities.

Sa Pedrissa, Deià
MAP C2 ▪ Ctra Valldemossa-Deià, km 64.5 ▪ 971 639111 ▪ www.sapedrissa.com ▪ €€€
Surrounded by ancient olive trees and blessed with fabulous sea and mountain views, this 16th-century country estate has been restored to the high standards of the best boutique hotels, without losing its historic appeal. Guests can dine on excellent local cuisine in the beautiful converted olive-press room. Some areas offer wheelchair access.

Son Gener, Son Servera
MAP G3 ▪ Ctra Son Servera–Artà, Ma-4031, km 3 ▪ 971 183612 ▪ www.songener.com ▪ Closed Dec–mid-Jan ▪ €€€
This agroturismo is set in an exquisite 18th-century country estate with charm and personalized service. The cooking is top-notch, and all rooms are sleek junior suites. There are plenty of amenities too, including a golf course, a pool and a spa, as well as partial wheelchair access.

Monasteries, Refuges and Hostels

Albergue de Cabrera
MAP H6 ▪ 971 656282 ▪ www.cvcabrera.es/ca/albergue-de-cabrera ▪ Closed Nov–Apr ▪ €
This refuge is the only accommodation available on the tiny island of Cabrera, a national park and marine wildlife reserve. Providing simple rooms and food, the place makes a wonderful base for exploring the beautiful and unspoiled archipelago.

Castell d'Alaró
MAP D3 ▪ Puig d'Alaró ▪ 971 182112 ▪ No credit cards ▪ No en-suite ▪ No air-con ▪ www.castellalaro.cat ▪ €
The hostel is a 45-minute walk from the car park and scenic castle (see p103). There are double and triple rooms and dorms, a snack bar and communal room, but facilities are modest: guests should bring everything they require. There is no wheelchair access.

Ermita de Bonany, Petra
MAP F4 ▪ Puig de Bonany ▪ 971 826568 ▪ No en-suite ▪ No air-con ▪ €
Set in a Special Interest Nature Area, this striking hermitage offers basic accommodation. The five rooms share communal showers, a kitchen, dining room and outside barbecue areas (bring your own) with picnic tables.

La Victoria Petit, Alcúdia
MAP F2 ▪ Ctra Cabo, Pinar, km 6 ▪ 971 549912 ▪ www.lavictoriahotel.com ▪ €
Dating back to the 1400s, this renovated hermitage welcomes visitors to stay in a few rooms. Though simple, these rooms are spotlessly clean and offer wonderful views of the sea. The location is a little remote, so it is best to have a car if you want to get into nearby Alcúdia.

Petit Hotel Santuari de Sant Salvador, Felanitx
MAP F5 ▪ Pl. Santa Margarita, 6 ▪ 971 515260 ▪ No air-con ▪ www.santsalvadorhotel.com ▪ €
Modest, but welcoming en-suite accommodation

(see p44). Amenities include hot water, a kitchen, a dining room, barbecue areas, picnic tables, a bar and a restaurant.

Santuari de Cura, Randa
MAP E4 ▪ Randa, 07629 ▪ 971 120260 ▪ No air-con ▪ www.santuaridecura.com ▪ €
Set in verdant, peaceful gardens on the peak of the Puig de Randa, this historic sanctuary offers far-reaching views across the island. Beautifully restored, the rooms are comfortable and well equipped, and the restaurant serves great food.

Santuari de Lluc
MAP D2 ▪ Pl. dels Peregrins, 1 ▪ 971 871525 ▪ www.lluc.net ▪ No air-con ▪ €
The most famous of Mallorca's retreats (see pp30–31) offers guests considerable comfort and every sort of facility, including outside tables, barbecue areas, bars, three restaurants, and even several camping options. Wheelchair access is limited.

Santuari de Monti-Sion, Porreres
MAP E4 ▪ Oratori de Monti-Sion ▪ 971 647185 ▪ Closed Aug ▪ No credit cards ▪ No air-con ▪ €
The very simple amenities here are reminiscent of the asceticism of the past. The 16th-century lecture hall is preserved, as are four Gothic pillars on the path that ascends from the village to the summit. There are great views of the Es Pla. The sanctuary has no amenities for guests with specific needs.

General Index

Acknowledgments

Author
Jeffrey Kennedy is a freelance travel writer who divides his time between the Iberian Peninsula, Italy and the USA. He is the author of DK's *Top 10 Miami* and *Top 10 San Francisco* and co-author of *Top 10 Rome*.

Additional contributor
Mary-Ann Gallagher

Publishing Director Georgina Dee

Publisher Vivien Antwi

Design Director Phil Ormerod

Editorial Sophie Adam, Ankita Awasthi Tröger, Rachel Fox, Freddie Marriage, Sally Schafer

Cover Design Maxine Pedliham, Vinita Venugopal

Design Tessa Bindloss, Ankita Sharma

Picture Research Taiyaba Khatoon, Sumita Khatwani, Ellen Root, Rituraj Singh

Cartography Subhashree Bharti, Tom Coulson, Martin Darlison, James Macdonald

DTP Jason Little

Production Poppy Werder-Harris

Factchecker Phil Lee

Proofreader Clare Peel

Indexer Helen Peters

Revisions Avanika, Mohammad Hassan, Shikha Kulkarni, Bandana Paul, Priyanka Thakur, Stuti Tiwari, Tanveer Abbas Zaidi

Commissioned Photography
Ian Aitken, Suzanne Porter, Colin Sinclair

First edition created by Blue Island Publishing, London

Picture Credits
The publisher would like to thank the following for their kind permission to reproduce their photographs:
(**Key:** a-above; b-below/bottom; c-centre; f-far; l-left; r-right; t-top)

123RF.com: jcv 49tr; Igor Plotnikov 54tr; romasph 44b, 121bl; Florian Schtz 112b; Antonio Balaguer Soler 62b; Victor Pelaez Torres 57tl.

4Corners: Reinhard Schmid 34-5; SIME / Stefano Scatà 73br; Richard Taylor 44tl, 95cl.

Adrián Quetglas: 78ca.

Alamy Stock Photo: age fotostock 7tr, 20-1, 21tl, 30cl, 33tl, 37br, 50tl, 76bl, 83cla; Agencja Fotograficzna Caro 35tr; Alltravel 11tl; Bon Appetit 76cr; Oliver Brenneisen 79tl, 125br; CFimages 75crb; Colau 82tl, 87br; Carl DeAbreu 10cl; Carlos Dominique 86tl; dpa picture alliance archive 45tr, / Alexandra Schuler 36clb; Greg Balfour Evans 84-5, 96br; F1online digitale Bildagentur GmbH 84tl; Kevin George 79cra; Elly Godfroy 124cra; Susana Guzman 26-7, 30-1; Peter Hollbaum-Hansen 28br; Hemis 14cr, 74tl, 78br, 130cl; imageBROKER 28cl, 47tr, 52tl, 88bl, 96cla, 105tl; David Kilpatrick 10clb, 20bl, 21cr; LAR Cityscapes 73t; Chlaus Loetscher 43br; LOOK Die Bildagentur der Fotografen GmbH 83br, 98tl; Johnny Madsen 110c; Mallorcalmages 98crb; mauritius images GmbH 15b; Graham Mulrooney 93br; Naeblys 30br; Dave Porter 127br; Robertharding 68cl, Pep Roig 68bl; Andreas Rose 4cla; Matthias Scholz 51tr; Axel Schweiss 66-7; Skim New Media Limited 23cr; 77tr; Boris Stroujko 2tl, 8-9; Paolo Trovò 62tl; Dieter Wanke 48cr; Tim Wright 25bl; Zoonar GmbH 122ca.

AWL Images: Michele Falzone 13crb, 58bl, 93tr; Katja Kreder 32cla, 63cl.

Banana Club: 114br.

Bodegues Ribas: 82b.

Cala Gran Cocktail Bar: 124cr

Casino de Mallorca: 74b.

Cuit, Palma: 99br.

Depositphotos Inc: castenoid 4cl, 102t; PBphotos 56b.

Dreamstime.com: Aldorado10 49b, 60t, 104clb, 110b; Alejphoto 65tr; Allard1 3tr, 119tr; 128-9, 132-3; Americanspirit 129cla; Artesiawells 10crb, 29cra, 50br, 54clb, 89br; Balakate 68t; Yulia Belousova 92tl; Blurf 71cl; Nonglak Bunkoet 108bl; Yevgen Byelykh 11clb; Davidwind 10br; Kevin Eaves 103cl; Fotoandvideo 116-7; Harryfn 86br; Inge Hogenbijl 85tr, Ihb 17br; Isselee 25cl; Rainer Junker 7br; Gerd Kohlmus 42b; Lunamarina 11br, 61cr, 64bl, 77br, 118ca; Anna Lurye 55b; Markusbeck 32cr, 58t; Puri Martínez 6cla; Martinmates 37tl; Dmitri Maruta 11cr, 32-3; Juan Moyano 2tr, 38-9, 43cl; Alexander Nikiforov 16clb, 16-7, 120cl; Sean Pavone 22-3; Ppy2010ha 76tl; Rangzen 22crb; Richair 108tl; Romasph 57crb; Saaaaa 94t, 119b; Florian Schuetz 69br; Vampy1 4cr, 52crb, 109tr; Piotr Wawrzyniuk 34br; Xantana 10cra, 100cla, 101tl.

Es Fum, Costa d'en Blanes: 78b.

Fundació Pilar i Joan Miró: archive 18-9c; © DACS 2017 18cla, 18bc, Gabriel Lacomba 19br.

Fundación Yannick y Ben Jakober: 53b, 86c.

Getty Images: Gonzalo Azumendi 42tl, 87tl; Tolo Balaguer 23bl; DEA / G. Dagli Orti 41tr;

Europa Press 69tr; Hulton Deutsch 41bl; Holger Leue 70b, 72tl; PHAS 40crb; David C Tomlinson 11tr, 64t, 127tl; ullstein bild 31br; Hans Henning Wenk 88tr.

Goli Cafe é, Santanyi: 78t, 123cr.

iStockphoto.com: aldorado10 13bl; Alex 1; CamiloTorres 12cl; castenoid 24t; cinoby 4b; foto-select 12-3c; Khrizmo 4t; LUNAMARINA 4clb; pixelpot 111tl; raeva 36-7; RolfSt 28-9; Juergen Sack 4crb, 120-1, 122b; Satilda 3tl, 90-1; stocknshares 59br.

Karting Magaluf: 72c.

Restaurante Agapanto: 107cla.

Rialto Living, Palma: 97t.

Robert Harding Picture Library: Tom Mueller 23tl; Stella 126tl; Ruth Tomlinson 101b; Konrad Wothe 70tl, 102bl; Michael Zegers 46bl.

Scubar, Santa Ponça: 106clb.

Restaurant Stay: 115cla.

SuperStock: age fotostock 63br, / Carlos José Pache 65bl, / Tolo Balaguer 34cla, 40tl, 89clb, 131br; imageBROKER 127c, / Helmut Corneli 106tr; Westend61 / Martin Moxter 17bl.

Zaranda: 79crb.

Cover

Front and spine: **iStockphoto.com:** Alex. Back: **iStockphoto.com:** Alex b, cla, Josep Bernat Sànchez Moner crb, Juergen Sack tr; **Robert Harding Picture Library:** Purcell-Holmes tl.

Pull Out Map Cover

iStockphoto.com: Alex.

All other images © Dorling Kindersley
For further information see: www.dkimages.com

Penguin
Random
House

Produced by Blue Island, London

Printed and bound in China

First edition 2003

Published in Great Britain
by Dorling Kindersley Limited
80 Strand, London WC2R 0RL

Published in the United States by
DK US, 1450 Broadway, Suite 801,
New York, NY 10018, USA

Copyright © 2003, 2020 Dorling
Kindersley Limited

A Penguin Random House Company

19 20 21 22 10 9 8 7 6 5 4 3 2 1

Reprinted with revisions 2005, 2007, 2009, 2011, 2013, 2015, 2018, 2020

All rights reserved. No part of this publication may be reproduced, stored in or introduced into a retrieval system, or transmitted in any form, or by any means (electronic, mechanical, photocopying, recording or otherwise) without the prior written permission of the copyright owner.

A CIP catalogue record is available from the British Library.

A catalogue record for this book is available from the Library of Congress.

ISSN 1479-344X

ISBN 978-0-2414-0867-4

SPECIAL EDITIONS OF DK TRAVEL GUIDES

DK Travel Guides can be purchased in bulk quantities at discounted prices for use in promotions or as premiums. We also offer special editions and personalized jackets, corporate imprints, and excerpts from all our books, tailored specifically to meet your needs.

To find out more, please contact:

in the US
specialsales@dk.com
in the UK
travelguides@uk.dk.com
in Canada
specialmarkets@dk.com
in Australia
**penguincorporatesales@
penguinrandomhouse.com.au**

*As a guide to abbreviations in visitor information blocks: **Adm** = admission charge; **D** = dinner; **L** = lunch.*

MIX
Paper from
responsible sources
FSC™ C018179

English-Mallorquín Phrase Book

In an Emergency

Help!	Auxili!	ow-*gzee*-lee
Stop!	Pareu!	*pah*-reh-oo
Call a doctor!	Telefoneu un metge!	teh-leh-fon-*eh*-oo oon *meh*-djuh
Call an ambulance!	Telefoneu una ambulància!	teh-leh-fon-*eh*-oo oo-nah ahm-boo-*lahn*-see-ah
Call the police!	Telefoneu la policia	teh-leh-fon-*eh*-oo lah poh-lee-*see*-ah
Call the fire brigade!	Telefoneu els bombers!	teh-leh-fon-*eh*-oo uhlz boom-*behs*
Where is the nearest telephone?	On és el teléfon més proper?	on-ehs uhl tuh-*leh* fon mehs proo-*peh*
Where is the nearest hospital?	On és l'hospital més proper?	on-*ehs* looss-pee-*tahl* mehs proo-*peh*

Communication Essentials

Yes	Sí	see
No	No	noh
Please	Per favor	pair fa-*vor*
Thank you	Gràcies	*grah*-see-uhs
Excuse me	Perdona	puhr-*thoh*-na
Hello	Hola	*oh*-lah
Goodbye	Adéu	ah-*they*-oo
Good night	Bona nit	*bo*-nah neet
Morning	El matí	uhl mah-*tee*
Afternoon	La tarda	lah *tahr*-thuh
Evening	El vespre	uhl *vehs*-pruh
Yesterday	Ahir	ah-*ee*
Today	Avui	uh-*voo*-ee
Tomorrow	Demà	duh-*mah*
Here	Aquí	uh-*kee*
There	Allà	uh-*lyah*
What?	Qué?	keh
When?	Quan?	*Kwahn*
Why?	Per qué?	puhr keh
Where?	On?	ohn

Useful Phrases

How are you?	Com està?	kom uhs-*tah*
Very well, thank you.	Molt bé, gràcies.	mol beh *grah*-see-uhs
Pleased to meet you.	Molt de gust.	mol duh *goost*
See you soon.	Fins aviat.	feenz uhv-*yat*
That's fine.	Està bé.	uhs-*tah* beh
Where is/are … ?	On és/són… ?	ohn ehs/*sohn*
How far is it to…?	Quants metres/ kilòmetres hi ha d'aquí a … ?	kwahnz meh-truhs/kee-*loh*-muh-truhs yah dah-*kee* uh
Which way to … ?	Per on es va a … ?	puhr on uhs *bah* ah
Do you speak English?	Parla anglés?	*par*-luh an-*glehs*
I don't understand	No l'entenc.	noh luhn-*teng*
Could you speak more slowly, please?	Pot parlar més a poc a poc, si us plau?	pot par-*lah* mehs pok uh pok sees plah-*oo*
I'm sorry.	Ho sento.	oo *sehn*-too

Useful Words

big	gran	gran
small	petit	puh-*teet*
hot	calent	kah-*len*
cold	fred	fred
good	bo	boh
bad	dolent	doo-*len*
enough	bastant	bahs-*tan*
well	bé	beh
open	obert	oo-*behr*
closed	tancat	tan-*kat*
left	esquerra	uhs-*kehr*-ruh
right	dreta	*dreh*-tuh
straight on	recte	*rehk*-tuh
near	a prop	uh *prop*
far	lluny	*lyoon*yuh
up/over	a dalt	uh dahl
down/under	a baix	uh bah-*eeshh*
early	aviat	uhv-*yat*
late	tard	tahrt
entrance	entrada	uhn-*trah*-thuh
exit	sortida	soor-*tee*-thuh
toilet	lavabos/ serveis	luh-*vah*-boos sehr-*beh*-ees
more	més	mess
less	menys	men*yees*

Shopping

How much does this cost?	Quant costa això?	kwahn kost ehs-*shoh*
I would like …	M'agradaria …	muh-grah-*thuh*-ree-uh
Do you have?	Tenen?	*tehn*-un
I'm just looking, thank you	Només estic mirant, gràcies.	noo -mess ehs-*teek* mee-*rahn* *grah*-see-uhs
Do you take credit cards?	Accepten targes de crédit?	ak-*sehp*-tuhn tahr-*zhuhs* duh *kreh*-deet
What time do you open?	A quina hora obren?	ah *keen*-uh oh-ruh oo-*bruhn*
What time do you close?	A quina hora tanquen?	ah *keen*-uh oh ruh tan-*kuhn*
This one.	Aquest	ah-*ket*
That one.	Aquell	ah-*kehl*
expensive	car	kahr
cheap	bé de preu/ barat	beh thuh preh-oo/bah-*rat*
size (clothes)	talla/mida	*tah*-lyah/*mee*-thuh
size (shoes)	número	*noo*-mehr-oo
white	blanc	*blang*
black	negre	*neh*-gruh
red	vermell	vuhr-*mel*
yellow	groc	grok
green	verd	behrt
blue	blau	*blah*-oo
antiques shop	antiquari/ botiga d'antiguitats	an-tee-*kwah*-ree/boo-*tee*-gah/dan-tee-*ghee*-tats
bakery	el forn	uhl forn
bank	el banc	uhl bang
bookshop	la llibreria	lah lyee-bruh-*ree*-ah
butcher's	la carnisseria	lah kahr-nee-suh-*ree*-uh
fishmonger's	la peixateria	lah peh-shuh-tuh-*ree*-uh
greengrocer's	la fruiteria	lah froo-ee-tuh-*ree*-uh

grocer's	la botiga de queviures	lah boo-tee-guh duh keh-vee-oo-ruhs
hairdresser's	la perruqueria	lah peh-rroo-kuh-ree-uh
market	el mercat	uhl muhr-kat
newsagent's	el quiosc de premsa	uhl kee-ohsk duh prem-suh
pastry shop	la pastisseria	lah pahs-tee-suh-ree-ah
pharmacy	la farmàcia	lah fuhr-mah-see-ah
post office	l'oficina de correus	loo-fee-see-nuh duh koo-reh-oos
shoe shop	la sabateria	lah sah-bah-tuh-ree-uh
supermarket	el supermercat	uhl soo-puhr-muhr-kat
tobacconist's	l'estanc	luhs-tang
travel agency	l'agència de viatges	la-jen-see-uh duh vee-ad-juhs

Sightseeing

art gallery	la galeria d'art	lah gah-luh ree-yuh dart
cathedral	la catedral	lah kuh-tuh-thrahl
church	l'església/ la basílica	luhz-gleh-zee-uh/ lah buh-zee-lee-kuh
garden	el jardí	uhl zhahr-dee
library	la biblioteca	lah bee-blee-oo-teh-kuh
museum	el museu	uhl moo-seh-oo
tourist information office	l'oficina de turisme	loo-fee-see-nuh thuh too-reez-muh
town hall	l'ajuntament	luh-djoon-tuh-men
closed for holiday	tancat per vacances	tan-kat puhr bah-kan-suhs
bus station	l'estació d'autobusos	luhs-tah-see-oh dow-toh-boo-zoos
railway station	l'estació de tren	luhs-tah-see-oh thuh tren

Staying in a Hotel

Do you have a vacant room?	Tenen una habitació lliure?	teh-nuhn oo-nuh ah-bee-tuh-see-oh lyuh-ruh
double room with a double bed	habitació doble amb llit de matrimoni	ah-bee-tuh-see-oh doh-bluh am lyeet duh mah-tree-moh-nee
twin room	habitació amb dos llits/ amb llits individuals	ah-bee-tuh-see-oh am dohs lyeets/ am lyeets in-thee-vee-thoo-ahls
single room	habitació individual	ah-bee-tuh-see-oh een-dee-vee-thoo-ahl
room with a bath	habitació amb bany	ah-bee-tuh-see-oh am bahn-yuh
shower	dutxa	doo-chuh

porter	el grum	uhl groom
key	la clau	lah klah-oo
I have a reservation	Tinc una habitació reservada	ting oo-nuh ah-bee-tuh-see-oh reh-sehr-vah-thah

Eating Out

Have you got a table for …?	Tenen taula per …?	teh-nuhn tow-luh puhr
I would like to reserve a table.	Voldria reservar una taula.	vool-dree-uh reh-sehr-vahr oo-nuh tow-luh
The bill, please.	El compte, si us plau.	uhl kohm-tuh sees plah-oo
I am a vegetarian.	Sóc vegetarià/ vegetariana.	sok buh-zhuh-tuh-ree-ah buh-zhuh-tuh-ree-ah-nah
waitress	cambrera	kam-breh-ruh
waiter	cambrer	kam-breh
menu	la carta	lah kahr-tuh
fixed-price menu	menú del dia	muh-noo thuhl dee-uh
wine list	la carta de vins	lah kahr-tuh thuh veens
glass of water	un got d'aigua	oon got dah-ee-gwah
glass of wine	una copa de vi	oo-nuh ko-pah thuh vee
bottle	una ampolla	oo-nuh am-pol-yuh
knife	un ganivet	oon gun-ee-veht
fork	una forquilla	oo-nuh foor-keel-yuh
spoon	una cullera	oo-nuh kool-yeh-ruh
breakfast	l'esmorzar	les-moor-sah
lunch	el dinar	uhl dee-nah
dinner	el sopar	uhl soo-pah
main course	el primer plat	uhl pree-meh plat
starters	els entrants	uhlz ehn-tranz
dish of the day	el plat del dia	uhl plat duhl dee uh
coffee	el café	uhl kah-feh
rare	poc fet	pok fet
medium	al punt	ahl poon
well done	molt fet	mol fet

Menu Decoder

l'aigua mineral	lah-ee-gwuh mee-nuh-rahl	mineral water
sense gas/ amb gas	sen-zuh gas/ am gas	still/ sparkling
al forn	ahl forn	baked
l'all	lahlyuh	garlic
l'arròs	lahr-roz	rice
les botifarres	lahs boo-tee-fah-rahs	sausages
la carn	lah karn	meat
la ceba	lah seh-buh	onion
la cervesa	lah-sehr-ve-sah	beer
l'embotit	lum-boo-teet	cold meat
el filet	uhl fee-let	sirloin
el formatge	uhl for-mah-djuh	cheese
fregit	freh-zheet	fried
la fruita	lah froo-ee-tah	fruit
els fruits secs	uhlz froo-eets seks	nuts
les gambes	lahs gam-bus	prawns

el gelat	uhl djuh-*lat*	ice cream
la llagosta	lah lyah-*gos*-tah	lobster
la llet	lah *lyet*	milk
la llimona	lah lyee-*moh*-nah	lemon
la llimonada	lah lyee-moh-*nah*-thuh	lemonade
la mantega	lah mahn-*teh*-gah	butter
el marisc	uhl muh-*reesk*	seafood
la menestra	lah muh-*nehs*-truh	vegetable stew
l'oli	*loll*-ee	oil
les olives	luhs oo-*lee*-vuhs	olives
l'ou	*loh*-oo	egg
el pa	uhl *pah*	bread
el pastís	uhl pahs-*tees*	pie/cake
les patates	lahs pah-*tah*-tuhs	potatoes
el pebre	uhl *peh*-bruh	pepper
el peix	uhl *pehsh*	fish
el pernil salat serrà	uhl puhr-*neel* suh-*lat* sehr-*rah*	cured ham
el plàtan	uhl *plah*-tun	banana
el pollastre	uhl poo-*lyah*-struh	chicken
la poma	la *poh*-mah	apple
el porc	uhl *pohr*	pork
les postres	lahs *pohs*-truhs	dessert
rostit	rohs-*teet*	roast
la sal	lah *sahl*	salt
la salsa	lah *sahl*-suh	sauce
les salsitxes	lahs sahl-*see*-chuhs	sausages
sec	*sehk*	dry
la sopa	lah *soh*-puh	soup
el sucre	uhl-*soo*-kruh	sugar
la taronja	lah tuh-*rohn*-djuh	orange
el te	uhl *teh*	tea
les torrades	lahs too-*rah*-thuhs	toast
la vedella	lah veh-*theh*-lyuh	beef
el vi blanc	uhl *bee* blang	white wine
el vi negre	uhl *bee* neh-gruh	red wine
el vi rosat	uhl *bee* roo-*zaht*	rosé wine
el vinagre	uhl bee-*nah*-gruh	vinegar
el xai/el be	uhl *shahee*/ uhl *beh*	lamb
la xocolata	lah shoo-koo-*lah*-tuh	chocolate
el xoriç	uhl shoo-*rees*	red sausage

Numbers

0	zero	*seh*-roo
1	un (masc)	*oon*
	una (fem)	*oon*-uh
2	dos (masc)	*dohs*
	dues (fem)	*doo*-uhs
3	tres	*trehs*
4	quatre	*kwa*-truh
5	cinc	*seeng*
6	sis	*sees*
7	set	*set*
8	vuit	*voo*-eet
9	nou	*noh*-oo
10	deu	*deh*-oo
11	onze	*on*-zuh
12	dotze	*doh*-dzuh
13	tretze	*treh*-dzuh
14	catorze	kah-*tohr*-dzuh
15	quinze	*keen*-zuh
16	setze	*set*-zuh
17	disset	dee-*set*
18	divuit	dee-voo-*eet*
19	dinou	dee-*noh*-oo
20	vint	*been*
21	vint-i-un	been-tee-*oon*
22	vint-i-dos	been-tee-*dohs*
30	trenta	*tren*-tah
31	trenta-un	*tren*-tah oon
40	quaranta	kwuh-*ran*-tuh
50	cinquanta	seen-*kwahn*-tah
60	seixanta	seh-ee-*shan*-tah
70	setanta	seh-*tan*-tah
80	vuitanta	voo-ee-tan-tah
90	noranta	noh-*ran*-tah
100	cent	sen
101	cent un	sent oon
102	cent dos	sen dohs
200	dos-cents (masc)	dohs-sens
	dues-centes (fem)	*doo*-uhs sen-*tuhs*
300	tres-cents	trehs-senz
400	quatre-cents	kwah-truh-senz
500	cinc-cents	seeng-senz
600	sis-cents	sees-senz
700	set-cents	set-senz
800	vuit-cents	voo-eet-senz
900	nou-cents	noh-oo-cenz
1,000	mil	meel
1,001	mil un	meel oon

Time

one minute	un minut	oon mee-*noot*
one hour	una hora	oo-nuh oh-ruh
half an hour	mitja hora	mee-juh oh-ruh
Monday	dilluns	dee-*lyoonz*
Tuesday	dimarts	dee-*marts*
Wednesday	dimecres	dee-meh-kruhs
Thursday	dijous	dee-*zhoh*-oos
Friday	divendres	dee-*ven*-druhs
Saturday	dissabte	dee-*sab*-tuh
Sunday	diumenge	dee-oo-*men*-juh